PÂTÉS
FOR KINGS
AND COMMONERS

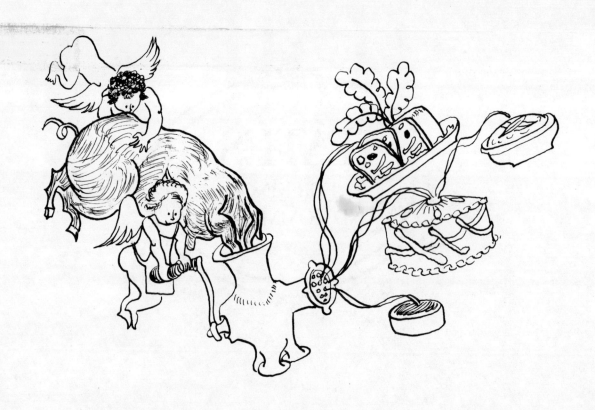

PÂTÉS

FOR KINGS AND COMMONERS

A Cookbook

by Maybelle Iribe and Barbara Wilder

Drawings by Maybelle Iribe

HAWTHORN BOOKS, INC.
Publishers / New York
A Howard & Wyndham Company

A special thanks to our learned friend John Dryden Movius, who graciously consented to write the extremely informative section, "Wines with Pâtés." A highly qualified author, he is editor of the *Wine Scene* consumer newsletter, instructor of all accredited wines courses at the University of California at Los Angeles, wine judge at the Los Angeles County Fair, and a founding member of Les Amis du Vin.

This volume is gratefully dedicated to

Sid
Lyn
Mary Helen
Lowell
Myles

and all the passionate lovers of pâté

Contents

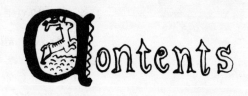

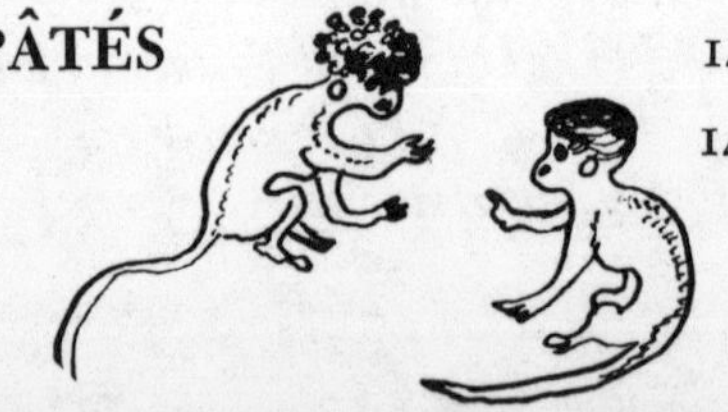

Authors' Notes

THE thought of some day writing a cookbook of great regional pâtés came to us soon after we first met in France over fifteen years ago. We discussed this project over several glasses of local champagne at Maybelle's eighteenth-century mill in Savigny and subsequently, we started gathering recipes for what we hoped would be a book dedicated to the French pâté, with variations from all the provinces of France. After living twenty-five years in Paris, Maybelle moved to California, and our long-awaited dream became a reality.

We both were a bit fearful that our French recipes might be difficult to translate into the American vernacular, but after careful research and practice we can assure you that simplicity and ease are the keynotes of our pâté recipes. They have been updated for American kitchens and a "dash" of this or a "soupçon" of that have been standardized. Many of these recipes were never written out before, and existed only in the memories of village housewives or had been passed along in families from mother to daughter. These are authentic regional pâtés in all their original splendor.

We both want to share our passion for pâtés with you, in the hope that they will become an integral part of your special food world.

Maybelle Iribe and Barbara Wilder

Meet the Pâté

THE PÂTÉ truly is a wonderful and versatile creation. It can be the perfect way to introduce a dinner to two or two hundred. Accompanied by a green salad and little cornichon pickles, it adds style to any luncheon and elegance to any picnic. And cut into bite-size squares and accompanied by French bread, it can make even the most sophisticated gourmand forget about caviar and conventional hors d'oeuvres, turning an ordinary cocktail party into a smashing event.

When we refer to pâté, we are definitely not thinking of the common chicken liver spread that immediately comes to mind, nor of pâté de foie gras, that ultimate French luxury (although we do include a recipe for it). Instead, we mean the whole glorious gamut of lusty and delicious concoctions filling the windows of the charcuteries (shops selling pâtés and the different specialities made from the pig) in every corner of France.

This book is going to try to teach you, step by simple step, how to make many different kinds of real French pâtés, with a nod to their English and American cousins. In addition, we will show you how to eat them with gusto and make them an important part of your menu planning. Believe us, if you can make a meat loaf, the great American standby, you can certainly make any of our pâtés.

We hope you will come to love this rather unknown and heretofore little appreciated culinary art form, and use our recipes; they were gathered during the many years we lived in France and then adapted for today's kitchen.

1

Centuries of Pâtés

THE PÂTÉ'S glorious history seems to have commenced during the early Middle Ages. Possibly a nobleman took too many ducks, geese, peacocks, pheasants, swans, larks, or whatever home to his castle, giving orders to turn them into something more that the usual roast-on-the-spit supper. Or he may requested them baked in a pie, since references to "pasties" date from the medieval era in England. Another supposition is that teeth were not very strong in those days because of the consumption of meat and pastry; vegetables were for the commoners. Consequently, our lord may have wished his food hashed or minced. Actually, the creator of the pâté also could have been a man of the cloth; records dating from the fourteenth century show that papal pâtés took on all sorts of spectacular shapes and sizes. Cockatrices (the front half of one animal and the back half of another stuffed with forcemeat, then sewn together) adorned with heads, tails and feathers were the greatest novelties of these enormous feasts. But whatever the version, pâtés were on their way halfway through the Middle Ages.

During the fifteenth century, King René imported the partridge from the Greek island of Chios and now is credited with the invention of the partridge pâté. During the previous century, the royal chef Taillevent gives us a recipe for a pheasant pâté.

Early in the sixteenth century, Henry III of France could be seen savoring his pâtés, dressed in the fashion of the day, ruff around his neck, and a ruffled tablecloth to match. A book comes to us from that time, *1,000 Ways to Prepare Birds*. Poultry pâtés were among the favorite dishes to "... set before the king"—meat had fallen from favor and fowl was in.

The Renaissance, of course, brought about changes in cuisine, thanks to Catherine and Marie de Médicis and their introduction of Italian chefs. The clever French accepted the chefs gracefully, since they knew they could learn many new dishes. Thanks to the Italians, meat was given another chance, this time accompanied by tantalizing sauces, which seduced even the most jaded court palates.

The only dropout of that century was Henry IV, who had simpler tastes. Although he loved garlic, he was content to feed on rather bland "chicken in the pot." Henry's lack of interest in exotic dining habits seems even more unusual when one considers the fact that he was conceived after his father had partaken of a particularly delicious truffled liver pâté! One can find as many as five meat pâtés and even an artichoke pâté on a sixteenth century menu.

Seventeenth century dinners during the reign of the Sun King, Louis XIV, were truly spectacular, and Louis's appetites are legendary. Menus featured hot pâtés as first and second courses (pâté of boned capon with musk or the Sun King golden pigeon pâté, served on a bed of unctuous green peas). Those were the days! Banquets teemed with as many as a thousand guests, who dined on endless courses and offerings.

This incredible feasting continued throughout the eighteenth century, perhaps palling with the lackluster appetite of the son of Louis XIV However, complicated and

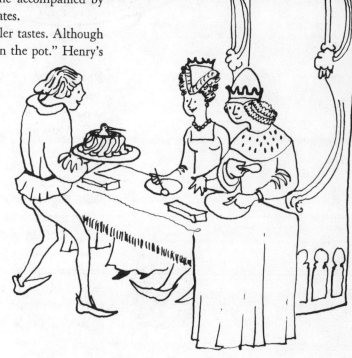

elaborate pâtés en croûte were created to tempt the king, and they undoubtedly found their way onto the menu of France's first real restaurant, which opened its doors in Paris around 1767.

The Duke de Richelieu and later Talleyrand certainly used their laden tables most effectively to further the cause of French diplomacy. By then, the pâté en croûte was being decorated with whatever symbol of nobility was needed to impress their elitist guests. Fleurs-de-lys and Napoleon's imperial bee were changed back and forth, depending on who was in power.

The approach of the nineteenth century saw more and more restaurants opening, as the chefs of noble Frenchmen found themselves out of work during and after the Revolution. Dinners started becoming intimate affairs, with Brillat-Savarin in his *Physiologie du Goût* recommending that a "perfect meal should be served to no more than twelve guests." He also gave advice on the perfect room temperature for serving wine and food to those present—sixty-one to sixty-six degrees Fahrenheit. A bit chilly by our present standards.

Wines played an ever-increasing role in the later centuries, eclipsing the hearty ales and meads of medieval times. Burgundy and Bordeaux began to celebrate their annual crops of grapes. Eventually, every course of a French meal was accompanied by an appropriate wine. Pâtés particularly have enjoyed the tradition of a wine companion. A glass of red or rosé wine with a pâté is a perfect marriage and a *must*.

Today pâtés are part of the French life-style. We hope with these recipes that you, too, can easily learn how to make pâtés a part of yours.

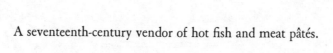

A seventeenth-century vendor of hot fish and meat pâtés.

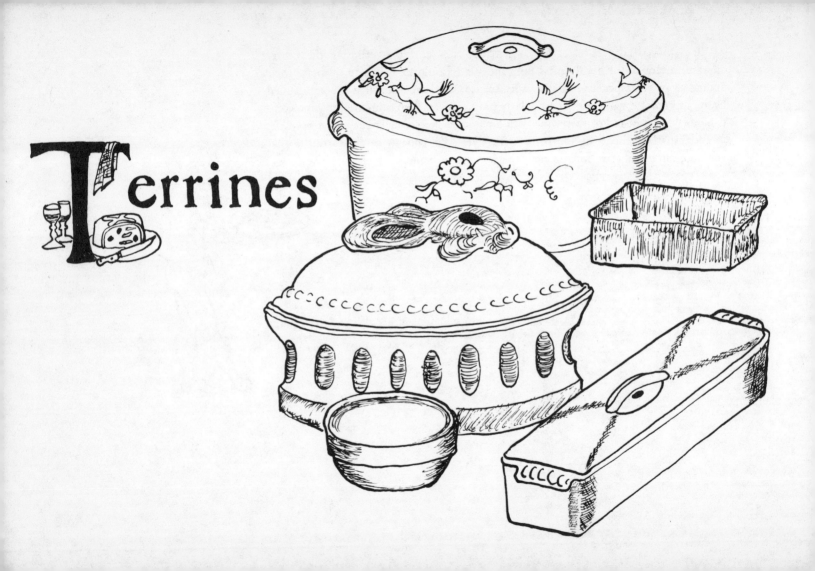

Terrines

The Proper Tools

ORE beautiful serving dishes have been made for the pâté than for any other French creation. Terrines range from downright sumptuous and extravagantly expensive to relatively cheap. You still can find lovely vestiges of pâté terrines in antique shops across the country, but fortunately, and with equal ease, you are able to buy sensible, undecorated ones that do honor to any table. Decorative terrines continue to be made with lids shaped like duck, pheasant, or rabbit heads, and these really should be used for those particular types of pâtés. However, the handsome, undecorated white porcelain ones and the rustic pottery dishes leave everything up to your own genius, and let's face it, it's what's inside that counts!

If you feel the need to be daringly elegant, your pheasant pâté can look very fin de siècle in a white terrine, *if* you keep the head and the tail feathers of your pheasant in the freezer. Take them out at the last minute, put the head on one end of your pâté, and let the tail feathers swoosh over the other end.

We have made pâtés in every possible type of container except tin, which is used exclusively for pâté en croûte. Meat does not seem happy surrounded by this material and sometimes reflects this aversion by taking on a slightly "tinny" taste. Aluminum loaf pans from your supermarket are great to use for your first attempts, and we recommend them highly.

You will also need:

A large mixing bowl. Use a 4- to 6-quart size made of stainless steel, earthenware, or glass.

A spatula and a sturdy wooden spoon. These are necessary tools for mixing, if you don't feel like getting in there with your hands. We love to!

Large rectangular pans. You will need one or two of these to hold your pâté dishes in a hot water bath. We use a 15 x 10½ x 2½ for large terrines and a 13 x 9 x 2½ for aluminum loaf pans.

A sharp knife. We stress this item because you must have one to finely chop your pork, chicken or other livers and pare away unwanted little membranes or sinews. We know that good knives are expensive, but they last a lifetime and are well worth the initial investment. You will also need a sharpening steel to maintain a proper cutting edge. Even with the wonderful invention of food processors, such as the Cuisinart * machine, some things still have to be done by hand in order to yield perfect results. Besides, it's fun.

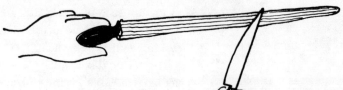

Once you have gathered together the aforementioned utensils, you will be properly equipped to tackle any pâté recipe in our book. Now, cast your aversions, prejudices, and fears to the wind and become adventuresome!

* CUISINART is a registered trademark of Cuisinarts, Inc.

"Pig, Admirable Animal— Veritable Meal on Feet"

MOTHER Nature's greatest gift to pâté-making is the pig . . . truly a glorious and unappreciated animal. *"De la tête à la queue, tout est bon"* ("Everything good from head to tail!"). This is so true. In America, the various lowly cuts of pork, such as melts, heart, liver, tripe, etc., are called specialty meats and are seldom used. The French have become masters at using these cuts and most of the great country cooking derives from them.

The fat of this animal plays a particularly big role in your pâtés. They should not be greasy, but fat must be added in the right proportions to preserve them. This protective fat around your slice of pâté is not to be eaten. The lovely, golden-yellow fat (*gras*) of the goose liver (*foie*) coats this famous pâté, preserving it for a long time. One of the great joys of pâté-making is its life span within your refrigerator, after baking. Because of the fat and brandy content, it can last for weeks. You can serve it to unexpected guests for an impromptu dinner, or depend on it for a party planned a couple of weeks ahead. Once you have perfected making pâtés, you will want to keep these faithful friends on hand in your refrigerator or freezer.

We do not want to become too lyrical about lace or caul fat, but here is another beautiful discovery in the learning process of pâté-making. Like gossamer, it is a thin membrane with weblike tracings of the purest white fat. This web surrounds the pig's stomach; after it has been soaked and cleaned, you will use it as a wrapping to gently lard the pâtés as they bake. Learn to use this product well, because there is no end to the wonderful dishes you can make with caul fat. It holds in all the succulent juices and automatically bastes everything for you. As it bakes, lace fat turns into a golden-brown coating for your pâtés of roasted chicken, rabbit, or kidney.

You should be able to order lace fat from your local butcher. It comes frozen, but don't be concerned since freezing does not change its qualities. To defrost, place in your refrigerator overnight or in a barely warm oven about one hour. Have your butcher wrap it in one or more packages for your freezer. Before you use fresh or defrosted lace fat, plunge it in a bowl of tepid water containing one teaspoon of vinegar. This can be done the night before you plan to make your pâtés. The next morning, keep changing the water by letting cold water run into the bowl. Do this until your lace fat is quite white. (It is originally rather pink). Dry it thoroughly and—voilà! It is ready for use. Certain pâtés, such as the Breton, should be wrapped in it, as they are not meant to be covered while cooking in the oven.

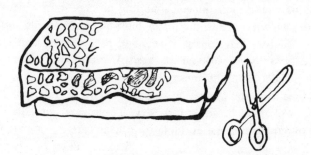

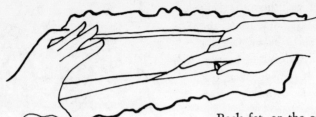

Back fat, on the other hand, consists of long strips of fat off the back of the pig. It is very white, with no tracings of meat. Ask your nice butcher to cut this into long, thin strips for wrapping around your pâtés. An alternative is to freeze it yourself, then slice it thinly on a meat slicer. Strips can be placed between sheets of waxed paper so that they do not touch each other, then frozen. It takes about one half hour to defrost these strips. They should be ready for use when you have put all your pâté ingredients together in your mixing bowl.

In most cookbooks, the base for every pâté is called *forcemeat*. We think that this term conjures up a most difficult-sounding process—one which is really very simple. Therefore, we will refer to the major bulk of ground meat and fat within a pâté as the base. The base may consist of veal and pork, or veal and fat, or ham and fat, or pork and fat (always pork fat, of course), ground together by your butcher. The above ingredients apply to meat pâtés.

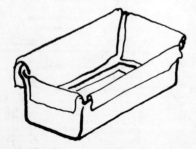

The "base" for the "lean" or fish pâté is quite different. It usually consists of proportions of milk, bread, and parsley. These vary with the different pâtés as you will see in our recipes. An example for a liver pâté de campagne begins with a base to which you add either whole duck, chicken, turkey, or goose livers, which have previously been marinated in a liquor of your choice. Sometimes a binder is necessary if the mixture is very soft. In these instances, an egg or bread crumbs can be added. Especially for delicate fish pâtés.

We don't anticipate your having any difficulty in obtaining the pork products listed above, but if you do, here are some substitutions:

> If *lace fat* is unobtainable, use the thin, white strips of *back fat*. If this, too, is hard to find, then lay pieces of *fatty bacon* on the bottom and sides of your pâté dish and wrap them over the top of the pâté.

As you begin to cook with these lowly and neglected pieces of pork, you will become aware of a truly unique and delicious taste transformation that takes place. Herein lies the art of Chinese and French cooking. An example of this creative simplicity or ingenuity is the charcutier of the Loire Valley in France, who takes pork "melts," ties them in lovely knots, and smokes them . . . delicious!

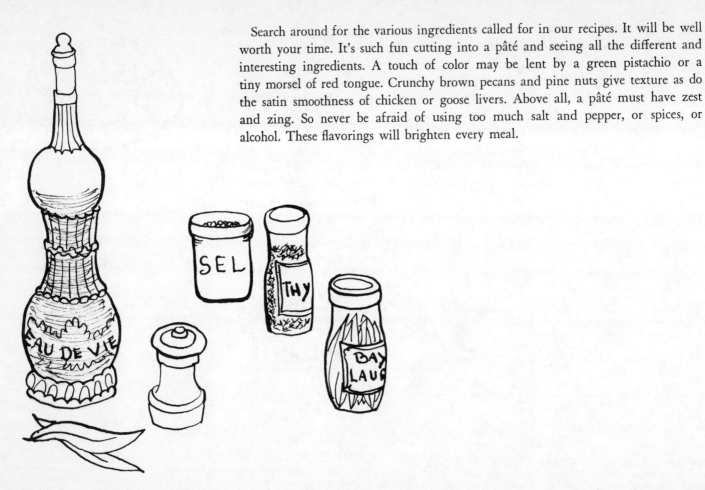

Search around for the various ingredients called for in our recipes. It will be well worth your time. It's such fun cutting into a pâté and seeing all the different and interesting ingredients. A touch of color may be lent by a green pistachio or a tiny morsel of red tongue. Crunchy brown pecans and pine nuts give texture as do the satin smoothness of chicken or goose livers. Above all, a pâté must have zest and zing. So never be afraid of using too much salt and pepper, or spices, or alcohol. These flavorings will brighten every meal.

14

The Provinces

La vie est belle

Sologne Pâtés

A beautifully engraved invitation with a little map showing the guests how to reach Rillerand used to arrive every autumn. It was part of a way of life. The host and hostess were elderly, but in good health. Both loved inviting their friends to their estate in the Sologne. Its forests and ponds were ideal for many varieties of game. Rabbit, after having nearly vanished from the rest of France, even found a haven here.

Their hunting lodge was lovely, and after a busy week in Paris it was always a great pleasure to arrive to complete calm, a roaring fire in the enormous living room, and these dear friends ever attentive and so kind. One's room remained the same, year after year, smelling of beeswax and lavender. Meals were perfection, prepared by the faithful Camille, who lived in a nearby farm on the property. She, too, was getting on in years. The weekend of shooting, walking, or just resting went by all too fast. It was always a sad goodbye.

Then one year there was no invitation. The host had passed away and our hostess did not have the heart to carry on there without him. She left the Sologne for their Paris home. Rillerand now belongs to their sons and their families.

The next shooting season there was painful and we knew our pleasure at Rillerand had not just been a visit to a beautiful estate in the Sologne, it had been the presence of an exceptional couple.

Here are some pâté recipes Camille let us copy. Incidently, she was very contemptuous of the famous Tatin sisters and their apple pie. "They invented nothing" she would say. "It is a very old pie in the Sologne called tarte à l'envers (upside down pie)."

TERRINE DE CANARD À L'ORANGE

PREPARATION:
30 minutes, plus 2 hours for marinating the duck breasts

COOKING TIME:
1¾ hours at 350°

INGREDIENTS:

 1 5-pound duck, with liver reserved
 ¾ cup port wine
 6 ounces cooked ham
 6 ounces lean veal
 ¾ pound pork fat
 ¾ pound chicken livers
 2 tablespoons butter
 2 shallots
 ½ teaspoon thyme
 1 large egg
 ⅓ cup bread crumbs
 2 teaspoons salt
 1 teaspoon freshly ground black pepper
 1 orange, sliced and with zest reserved
 1 thin piece of lace fat, large enough to line your pans or terrines

Aspic Jelly:
  1 envelope unflavored gelatin
  1½ cups cold chicken broth (for golden aspic) or
  1½ cups cold beef broth (for a darker-colored aspic)
  ¼ cup orange juice
  ¼ cup reserved port wine marinade

Garnishes:
Parsley sprigs
Laurel or bay leaves, truffle slices, orange slices, olives, or nuts (optional)

MAKES:

1 medium Pyrex loaf pan (8½ x 4½ x 2½) or 2 smaller loaf pans or terrines

METHOD:

Cut the duck breast into finger-length, half-inch slices (no skin) and reserve. Cut any other nice chunks from the duck and coarsely chop. Let them marinate at least 2 hours in the port wine. Meanwhile, grind the ham, veal, and pork fat in a Cuisinart or other processor. Sauté the reserved duck liver and chicken livers in the butter until slightly firm, then chop them into large pieces with a knife. Mix all the base meats together with the chopped shallots, thyme, egg, livers, breadcrumbs, 1 teaspoon of the salt, and ½ teaspoon of the pepper. Add the grated zest of half an orange. Add 3 tablespoons of the marinade and mix thoroughly. Set aside ¼ cup preserved marinade to be used in aspic jelly. Line the terrine or Pyrex loaf pan with the lace fat, draping it over the sides. Spread a layer of a third of base mixture, then a layer of half the duck pieces, then a third of the base meat, the rest of the duck pieces and then the last layer of the base meat, seasoning each layer with the remaining salt and pepper. Cover with the draped lace fat. Place the terrine, uncovered, in a hot-water bath in a large rectangle pan. Bake in a preheated 350° oven 1¾ hours. After you have removed the pâté from the oven, weight it down with a heavy plate and a can of tuna and allow it to cool. Refrigerate the pâté covered, until it is nice and cold.

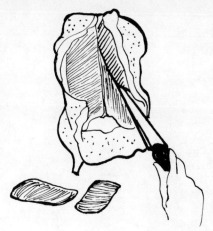

Aspic Jelly:
Soak the gelatin in ¼ cup of the cold chicken or beef broth. Stir until dissolved. Heat the remaining 1¼ cups chicken or beef broth with the orange juice and marinade until boiling. Add the gelatin mixture and stir well, until gelatin is completely dissolved. Chill the aspic in the refrigerator until it reaches the consistency of a thick syrup. When the aspic is thickened, use it in one of three ways:

1. Remove the pâté from the terrine and completely clean the terrine and wipe the pâté dry, removing the thin layer of lace fat around the pâté. Pour a little aspic on the bottom of the terrine and place several orange slices attractively on the bottom. Pour a little more aspic over the oranges and allow it to chill in the refrigerator until set. Then replace the pâté in the terrine and fill in around the sides with the aspic. Chill thoroughly and when ready to serve, place the terrine in hot water briefly, then unmold bottom side up. Decorate with parsley sprigs and serve.

2. Leave the pâté in the terrine after it has chilled. Remove the thin film of lace fat from the top of the cold pâté and pour the aspic over. Decorate the top with the orange slices and let it chill a bit more. Then pour more aspic over the terrine and allow it to chill completely. Serve the pâté in the terrine and slice it at the table.

3. If you wish to decorate your pâté with laurel or bay leaves, truffle slices, orange slices, olives, or nuts, quickly chill some of the aspic in a pie pan in the freezer until it is syrupy, then dip the decorations in the aspic and place on top of the pâté. Chill for a few minutes in the refrigerator to set the decorations, then pour the rest of the aspic over the top and the decoration will remain in place.

PHEASANT WITH TRUFFLES

PREPARATION:

1 hour

COOKING TIME:

1¾ hours at 350°

INGREDIENTS:

1 2½-to-3-pound pheasant, dressed
¾ to 1 pound lean pork and ¾ to 1 pound lean veal,
   which together weigh the same as the pheasant meat
⅔ cup brandy

¾ pound chicken livers, finely chopped

2 tablespoons butter

1 truffle, slivered, or ¼ pound mushrooms, finely sliced

6 ounces of pork fat

2 shallots, chopped

1 teaspoon salt

½ teaspoon freshly ground black pepper

1 thin piece of lace fat, large enough to line your terrine

1 laurel or bay leaf (optional)

MAKES:

1 small terrine (1 quart)

METHOD:

Take the meat off the pheasant. You should have about 2 pounds. Cut it into finger-length pieces and place in a bowl. Cut the lean veal and lean pork into finger-length pieces and place in the bowl together with the pheasant meat. Pour brandy over the meat just to cover and let it marinate 2 to 3 hours. Clean the chicken livers and sauté them in the butter until firm but still pink inside. Remove and reserve. Sauté the truffle slivers or mushroom slices in the same pan. When cooked, remove with a slotted spoon, reserving the juice in the pan for later use. Grind the pork fat, shallots, and chicken liver in a Cuisinart or other processor. Place in a bowl and add the reserved pan juices, salt, pepper, and ¾ of the truffle slivers or mushroom slices. Drain the pheasant, pork, and veal pieces. Place the lace fat in the terrine, draping it over the sides. Divide both the base meat (chicken livers, pork fat, shallots) and the pheasant, pork, and veal pieces into thirds. Begin layering with a third of the base meat, then a layer of the pork-veal-pheasant mixture. Sprinkle a few truffle slivers or mushroom slices on top. Spread another layer of base meat, then a layer of pork-veal-pheasant, more truffle slivers or mushroom slices. Finally add a top layer of the base meat, then a layer of pork-veal-pheasant, then more truffle slivers or mushroom slices. Season the top with salt and pepper. Decorate with a laurel or bay leaf, if you like, and pull up the lace fat hanging over the edges and cover the top. Press down to make a compact mass and place the terrine in a hot water bath in a large rectangular pan. Bake in a preheated 350° oven 1¾ hours. Remove and weigh down with a heavy plate and can of tuna until cool. Refrigerate at least 12 hours before serving.

RABBIT PÂTÉ CAMILLE

PREPARATION:

45 minutes

COOKING TIME:

3 hours at 300°

INGREDIENTS:

  1 rabbit (about 2 pounds), with liver reserved
  1 tablespoon butter

1 teaspoon salt

½ teaspoon freshly ground black pepper (scant)

4 slices fatty bacon

2 chicken livers

1 large or 2 small shallots, finely chopped

⅛ teaspoon allspice (scant)

¼ cup bread crumbs

2 large egg yolks

4 tablespoons brandy

1 thin (⅛″) slice back fat large enough to line a 3-cup terrine

¼ teaspoon thyme

1 laurel or bay leaf

½ cup all-purpose flour, combined with 5 tablespoons water in a paste

MAKES:

1 small terrine (3 cups)

METHOD:

Ask your butcher to cut the rabbit into rather large pieces or cut it up yourself. Cut the meat off the bones in chunks. Coarsely chop this meat and sauté in the butter for a few minutes. Lightly salt and pepper these pieces and set them aside. Prepare the base meat by cutting the fatty bacon into small pieces or grind it in a Cuisinart or other processor. Finely chop the rabbit liver and chicken livers. Place the base meat in a bowl and add the finely chopped shallots, the remaining salt and pepper, allspice, bread crumbs, egg yolks, brandy, and sautéd rabbit meat. Mix thoroughly. Line your terrine with thin slices of back fat, draping it over the sides. Spoon in the pâté mixture, pressing down well to make a compact mass. Sprinkle a little salt and pepper and the thyme over the top of the pâté. Add a laurel leaf for decoration and cover the top with the draped back fat. Put on the lid of the terrine and seal it with a paste made of flour and water. If you are using a pan, cover with aluminum foil, and poke a small hole on top with a knife to allow the steam to escape. Place the pan or terrine in a hot water bath in a large rectangular pan. Bake in a 300° oven for 3 hours. Remove from the oven and break the flour-and-water seal. Pour a little melted shortening over the top to seal the pâté. Weigh down with a heavy plate and a can of tuna and allow to cool completely. Refrigerate covered, or with a piece of aluminum foil over the top for 3 hours before serving. This pâté keeps very well for 2 to 3 weeks under proper refrigeration.

Loire Pâtés

Touraine is really "La Douce France" where French, almost feminine, softness is found everywhere. Its golden, hazy skies and the greys of the shimmering willows along the banks are mirrored in its lazy rivers. Its soft climate is perfect for all its wines and makes picnic outings a pleasure all year round. We arrived at our fifteenth-century mill one lovely November afternoon, in anticipation of the Toussaint holiday. The next day our nearest village was celebrating its annual blood sausage and charcuterie fair. Blood sausage stuffed with apples, making light and delicious and tantalizing pâtés, were offered in every stall—delicacies refined enough for kings but now available to every commoner.

According to legend, the wine grapes of this region were first planted by good St. Martin of Tours and his monks. We love the charming story of how St. Martin's donkey inadvertently played the important role of inventor of "pruning grape vines." Having been parked by his owner, who was conversing with his fellow monks, the hungry donkey ate a few vines. The monks were amazed the following year to find that they had twice as many grapes on these vines as before!

According to Rabelais, the perfect French spoken by the inhabitants of the Touraine is due to their consumption of Vouvray, Chinon, Gamay, and the other great wines of this region. "They rejoice the heart!"

VEAL PÂTÉ MAYBELLJ

PREPARATION:

15 minutes

COOKING TIME:

2 hours at 400°

INGREDIENTS:

  1 pound veal shoulder, ground
  1 pound pork sausage, ground
1¼ pounds chicken livers
  2 large eggs
  1 cup chopped parsley
  1 tablespoon salt
1½ teaspoons freshly ground black pepper
⅓ cup brandy
  1 cup bread crumbs, soaked in 1 cup milk
⅓ cup chopped shallots
⅛ teaspoon thyme
  1 thin slice back fat, large enough to line 1 medium loaf pan
     plus 1 small loaf pan or terrine
  1 laurel or bay leaf

MAKES:

1 medium pyrex loaf pan (8½ x 4½ x 2½) and 1 small loaf pan, such as the disposable aluminum type, or 1 small terrine (1 quart)

METHOD:

Ask your butcher to grind the veal and pork or do it yourself in a Cuisinart or other processor. Cut the chicken livers in halves. Combine the veal, pork sausage, chicken livers, eggs, parsley, 2½ teaspoons salt, 1 teaspoon pepper, brandy, bread crumbs and shallots. Mix thoroughly with your hands. Line the loaf pans or terrines with the back fat. Spoon in the meat mixture, pressing down to make a solid mass. Sprinkle with the remaining salt and pepper, and the thyme. Place the laurel or bay leaves in the center for decoration and lay two strips of back fat on the top crosswise. Place the loaf pans or terrines in a hot water bath in a large rectangular pan. Bake, covered, in a preheated 400° oven 2 hours. Check after about 1½ hours to see if the pâtés are browning properly. If they need to brown, remove the lids or aluminum foil and allow to brown. When they are done, remove from the oven and take off the lids. Place a heavy plate and a can of tuna on top to weigh down the pâtés in their fat and allow to cool. Refrigerate, covered, for at least 6 hours or until ready to serve.

PORK, HAM AND PISTACHIO PÂTÉ

PREPARATION:

30 minutes

COOKING TIME:

1½ hours at 400°

INGREDIENTS:

1 thin (⅛″) slice back fat, large enough to line your terrine and cover the pâté
¼ pound shelled pistachios
¾ pound pork sausage
1½ teaspoons thyme
2 teaspoons salt
1 teaspoon freshly ground black pepper
2 slices cooked ham (about ½ pound)
¾ pound lean pork, coarsely ground
1 laurel or bay leaf

MAKES:

1 terrine (3 to 4 cups)

METHOD:

Line the terrine with back fat. Blanch the pistachios by pouring boiling salted water over them, allowing them to sit in the water briefly. Remove the skins. Start at the bottom of the terrine and put in half the pork sausage, pressing down. Sprinkle half the pistachios over the sausage and a third of the thyme, salt and pepper. Next add a slice of ham, then all the ground lean pork. Sprinkle with more thyme, salt and pepper. Add another layer of ham, the rest of the pistachios; finish with a layer of the sausage. Sprinkle the remaining thyme, salt, and pepper on top. Decorate with the laurel or bay leaf and cover the pâté with strips of back fat. Place the terrine in a hot water bath in a large rectangular pan and bake, covered, in a 400° oven 1½ hours. Remove from the oven and take off the lid or aluminum foil. Weigh down with a heavy plate and can of tuna so that the pâté will settle into the fat in the terrine. Allow to cool. Place in the refrigerator for 24 to 48 hours before serving.

TERRINE OF PORK AND VEAL WITH ASPIC JELLY

PREPARATION:

20 minutes

COOKING TIME:

1½ hours at 350°

INGREDIENTS:

1¼ pounds lean pork, coarsely ground
1¼ pounds fatty shoulder of veal, coarsely ground
4 ounces pork fat, finely ground
2 large shallots, finely chopped
2½ teaspoons salt
1 teaspoon freshly ground black pepper
¼ teaspoon thyme
1 cup pecans or pine nuts
2 tablespoons brandy
1 laurel or bay leaf
1 thin (⅛″) slice back fat to line the terrine

Aspic Jelly:
1 envelope unflavored gelatin
1½ cups cold chicken broth
½ cup golden dry sherry or Madeira

½ medium yellow onion, sliced and separated into rings
1 carrot, cut into flowerets (see illustration)
Parsley sprigs

MAKES:

1 medium terrine (1½ quarts)

METHOD:

This pâté, which is quite easy to make, looks very attractive. Have the meats ground by your butcher or do them yourself in a food grinder or processor. Place the ground pork, veal, pork fat, shallots, most of the salt and pepper, pecans, brandy, and thyme in a bowl, and mix thoroughly. Line the terrine with the back fat, then add in the pâté mixture, pressing down well. Lightly salt and pepper, and place the laurel or bay leaf on the top for decoration. Place two strips of back fat crosswise on top and cover with the lid or aluminum foil. If using foil don't forget to make a small hole in it to allow steam to escape. Place the terrine or pan in a hot water bath in a large rectangular pan, and bake in a preheated 350° oven 1½ hours. If the pâté is not brown on top, bake a little longer with the lid off. Remove from the oven and take off the lid or foil. Weigh down with a heavy plate and a can of tuna until well cooled. Wrap in foil and refrigerate for 3 to 4 hours. When very well chilled, remove the pâté from the terrine, pat dry, and wash out the terrine.

Aspic Jelly:
Soak the gelatin in ¼ cup of the cold chicken broth. Stir until dissolved. Heat the remaining 1¼ cups chicken broth with the sherry or Madeira until boiling. Add the gelatin mixture and stir well, until the gelatin is completely dissolved. Chill the aspic in the refrigerator until it reaches the consistency of a thick syrup. Pour some of the aspic on the bottom of the terrine and decorate with the laurel leaf in the center surrounded by the onion rings and the carrot flowerets (see illustration). Return to the refrigerator until the aspic has set well, about 1 hour, then replace the pâté in the terrine and spoon more aspic around the edges. Refrigerate overnight. When ready to serve, set the terrine in hot water for about one minute. Quickly unmold on your serving platter and surround with the parsley sprigs.

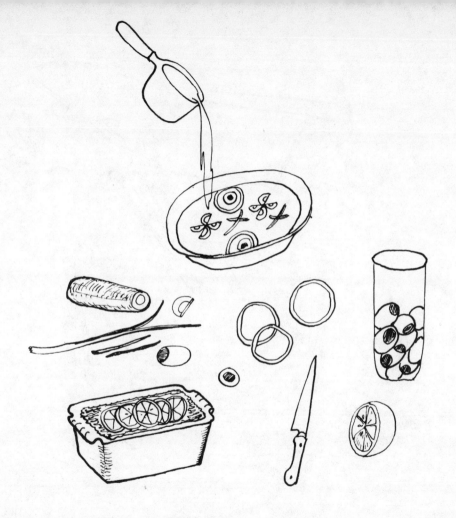

BURGUNDY PÂTÉ

"Burgundy" said Erasmus, "is a blessed province and should be called the mother of men, since she nurses them on such wonderful milk." He was speaking of her wines of course . . . the perfect complement to pâtés.

This province is also the home of other pâté accompaniments. Little Cornichon pickles grow like mad in its climate, and yellow mustard fields dot the countryside near Dijon.

The kind and portly former mayor of this city, the Abbot Kir invented a drink bearing his name, a wonderful combination of Cassis (black currant liquor) and white Burgundy. The basic recipe is one part Cassis to four parts white wine. (You can even make it with Champagne!) What a lovely, cool apéritif or picnic drink. Dijon has a glut of fabulous charcuteries and just what to buy is difficult to decide. Leaving these "gastronomical palaces" proved an ordeal, but finally we took our laden basket out on a country road, pulled over under a tree, in view of the ever present, heartwarming little vineyards, and feasted.

With a toast to Chanoine Kir with his "own," listen to our story of another of Burgundy's treasures, which came to light after sleeping in the Burgundian soil for more than 2,000 years: In January of 1953 a peasant from nearby Chatillon sur Seine, while plowing his field, unearthed these wonderful objects: a gold diadem and jewels belonging to a little princess of Gaul, a wheel of her funeral chariot, the bridle of a horse—and the Krater of Vix a gigantic Greek urn. How it ever found its way to this region in barbarian Gaul, by the side of the little princess, is unknown. We had the good fortune to see it in the Louvre a year later and again, a few years ago, back in its Burgundian home, the simple whitewashed, vaulted room of the Chatillon Museum. It is indeed a majestic object.

PÂTÉ PETITE PRINCESSE

PREPARATION:

15 minutes

COOKING TIME:

1¾ hours at 350°

INGREDIENTS:

1¼ pounds veal, coarsely ground
1¼ pounds beef, ground

1¼ pounds fatty shoulder of pork, coarsely ground
1 medium yellow onion, finely chopped
6 cloves garlic, crushed or finely chopped
2 large eggs
1 cup bread crumbs
4 teaspoons salt
2 teaspoons pepper
6 tablespoons brandy or ½ cup
1 thin (⅛″) slice back fat, large enough to line and top the loaf pans and terrine
1 laurel or bay leaf

MAKES:

2 medium Pyrex loaf pans (8½ x 4½ x 2½) or 2 medium disposable aluminum loaf
   pans (8½ x 4½ x 2½) plus 1 small terrine (3 cups)

METHOD:

Have your butcher grind the various meats or do it yourself with a Cuisinart unit
or other food processor. Chop the onion and garlic and put everything into a
bowl. Add the eggs, bread crumbs, most of the salt and pepper, and brandy, and mix
thoroughly. Line your pans or terrines with the very thinly sliced back fat and spoon
in the pâté mixture, pressing down to compact. Sprinkle with the remaining salt and
pepper, and decorate wtih the laurel or bay leaf. Place two strips of back fat crosswise on top of each pâté. Cover with the lids or alumium foil (don't forget the little
knife hole in the foil, for steam) and bake in a hot water bath in a large rectangular

pan in a preheated 350° oven 1¾ hours. Remove from the oven, weigh down with a plate and a can of tuna until cool. Refrigerate for at least 24 hours before serving or freeze when it is cold, if you prefer.

PÂTÉ MOUSSE WITH BACON

PREPARATION:

30 minutes

COOKING TIME:

10 to 12 minutes on top of the stove

INGREDIENTS:

Madeira Aspic:
  1 envelope unflavored gelatin
1½ cups chicken broth
½ cup Madeira

½ pound thickly sliced bacon
  1 pound chicken livers, cut into thirds
½ cup chopped scallions
½ cup Madeira

½ cup heavy cream
1 teaspoon salt
½ teaspoon freshly ground black pepper
¼ teaspoon thyme
⅛ teaspoon ground bay leaf
2 teaspoons lemon juice

Garnish:
1 truffle, sliced, 1 black olive, sliced, or 1 blanched almond, sliced

MAKES:

1 small terrine (3 cups) or 3 1-cup ramekins

METHOD:

This is a very smooth pâté with a delicious bacon-wine flavor. It makes excellent hors d'oeuvres served with thin slices of French bread.

Madeira Aspic:
Prior to making this pâté, we recommend that you make the Madeira Aspic and let it chill until ready to use. Soak the gelatin in ¼ cup of cold chicken broth. Stir until dissolved. Heat 1¼ cups chicken broth with ½ cup of Madeira to boiling. Add gelatin mixture and stir well until gelatin is completely dissolved. Allow the aspic to chill until the consistency of thick syrup so that it can be poured over and spooned around the various pâtés.

DO LAST, SO
TIME TO COOK LIV & BAC

Cut the thick bacon slices into one-inch pieces, and sauté in a skillet until the fat is rendered and the pieces are crisp but not burnt. Remove the bacon with a slotted spoon and reserve. Drain the bacon drippings and return ½ cup to the skillet. Add the chicken livers and scallions to the pan, and sauté for 2 to 3 minutes or until the livers are cooked but still pink inside. Pour the contents of the skillet into a bowl. Add the Madeira to the skillet and cook over moderately high heat until it is reduced to 3 tablespoons. Be sure all the nice brown bits are scraped up from the bottom of the pan. Add the heavy cream and simmer the mixture for one minute. Pour everything into the bowl with the livers and mix with a spoon. Put half the mixture plus half the bacon pieces into a Cuisinart or other processor and puree. Empty into a bowl and puree the remaining half of the liver mixture and bacon pieces, and also add them to the bowl. Season with the salt, pepper, thyme, ground bay leaf, and lemon juice. If you prefer more salt and pepper or more lemon juice, season to your taste. Pack the mixture into a 3-cup terrine or into smaller pots or dishes of your choice.

Once the pâté mixture is in the dish(es), decorate with truffle, black olive, or almond slices that have been dipped into the Madeira Aspic and allowed to set slightly. When set, pour the aspic over the top of the dish or dishes about ¼ inch thick. Refrigerate for several hours or overnight.

Auvergne

The Auvergne region has a chain of extinct volcanos, called *puys,* right down its middle. These long-dead monsters have a subsoil that resembles a sophisticated cigarette filter. Out of all these layers of pumice, rock, and sand bubbles forth some of the purest drinking water in the world. Hence, spas such as Vichy, the Mont-Dore, and Royat are located here and one can be certain of finding some of the best restaurants in France nearby.

With the countryside so beautiful, Auverge is also a perfect place for picnics. And, nearly every village has a great charcuterie filled with delicious pâtés and Auvergne hams hanging high. A slice of this and that, out we go, and into a cheese shop. More slices . . . some Cantal, perhaps a bleu d'Auvergne. Now for a bottle of Vichy. We can't decently buy anything else!

PÂTÉ DE CAMPAGNE D'AUVERGNE

PREPARATION:

20 minutes, plus refrigeration overnight

COOKING TIME:

1½ hours at 350°

INGREDIENTS:

1¾ pounds lean pork, cut into 1-inch cubes
½ pound pork fat, finely ground
½ pound beef, ground
 1 clove garlic
 1 large shallot
 4 tablespoons chopped parsley
 1 tablespoon salt
 2 teaspoons freshly ground black pepper
 1 teaspoon nutmeg
 2 tablespoons applejack or whiskey
½ cup all-purpose flour
 1 large egg
   Pinch of sugar
 1 thin slice lace fat, large enough to line the loaf pans or terrine
 1 laurel or bay leaf (optional)

MAKES:

2 medium disposable aluminum loaf pans (8½ x 4½ x 2½) or 1 medium terrine (1½ quarts)

METHOD:

Cut the pork into 1-inch cubes. Have your butcher grind the pork fat and beef or do it yourself with a Cuisinart or other processor. Place the meats in a large bowl. Chop the shallot, garlic, and parsley by hand or in a Cuisinart, and add to the meats. Add most of the salt and pepper, then the nutmeg, applejack or whiskey, flour, egg, and sugar, and mix thoroughly. Let it sit covered, overnight in the refrigerator. Line your terrine or aluminum pans with lace fat, letting the fat drape over the sides. Fill with pâté mixture and press down to make it compact. Sprinkle more salt and pepper over the top. Decorate with a laurel leaf if you like and cover the top with the hanging lace fat. Place loaf pans or terrine in a hot water bath in a large rectangular pan. Bake in a preheated 350° oven 1½ hours. Remove from oven and water bath and weigh down with a heavy plate and can of tuna. Allow the pâté to cool, about 2 hours, and then refrigerate until the fat has congealed, about 3 to 4 hours. Wrap for freezing or let sit for 24 to 48 hours to season before serving.

PÂTÉ CAMPAGNE MARCELLE I

PREPARATION:

30 minutes

COOKING TIME:

1¼ hours at 350°

INGREDIENTS:

  2 pounds lean pork, coarsely ground
1¾ pounds fatty shoulder of pork, ground
  2 pounds lean beef, ground
  3 tablespoons chopped parsley
1½ tablespoons salt
  1 tablespoon freshly ground black pepper
  1 cup bread crumbs soaked in 2 cups milk
  4 large eggs, lightly beaten
  3 tablespoons Pernod
  1 thin (⅛″) slice back fat, large enough to line 1 2-quart terrine or
    2 (8½ x 4½ x 2½) aluminum loaf pans
  2 teaspoons tarragon
  ½ cup all-purpose flour, combined with 5 tablespoons water

MAKES:

Approximately 7 pounds of pâté. This serves a crowd nicely, or you can cut this recipe in half.

METHOD:

Have your butcher grind the lean and fatty shoulder of pork or do it yourself with a Cuisinart or other processor. Place all ground meats in a large bowl and add the chopped parsley, salt and pepper, bread crumbs, eggs, and Pernod. Mix vigorously. Line your terrine or pans with your strips of thinly cut back fat. Add the pâté mixture to the terrine, pushing down to make it a compact mass. Decorate with the tarragon. Seal the cover with paste made of flour and water so that the steam escapes only from the little hole in the lid of the terrine or from the hole in your cover of aluminum foil. Place your terrine or aluminum loaf pan in a hot water bath, in a large rectangular pan. Bake in a preheated 350° oven 1¼ hours. Remove from oven, take off lid and weigh down with a heavy plate and can of tuna. Allow to cool, then refrigerate.

PÂTÉ CAMPAGNE MARCELLE II

PREPARATION:

20 minutes, plus refrigeration overnight

COOKING TIME:

1¾ hours at 350°

INGREDIENTS:

¾ pound pork fat, finely ground
1¾ pound lean pork, coarsely ground
1¾ pounds lean beef, regularly ground
3 medium yellow onions
¼ teaspoon ground cloves
1 tablespoon salt
½ tablespoon freshly ground black pepper
1½ teaspoons thyme
2 laurel leaves
4 tablespoons brandy
1 thin piece of lace fat, large enough to line the terrine and drape over

MAKES:

1 large terrine or casserole (2 quarts)

METHOD:

Have your butcher finely grind the pork fat, and coarsely grind the pork and beef or do it yourself in a Cuisinart or other processor. Put the fat and meats in a bowl. Grind the onions and add to the mixture in the bowl, along with the ground cloves and most of the salt, pepper, and thyme. Mix well. This mixture should be highly seasoned. Place your lace fat in the terrine, draping it over the sides. Spoon in the pâté mixture. Sprinkle the remaining salt, pepper and thyme lightly over the surface. Decorate with the laurel leaves and cover with the pieces of draped lace fat. Cover your terrine with its lid or aluminum foil. Punch a small hole with a knife in the foil to let the steam escape. Place in the hot water bath in a large rectangular pan and bake in a preheated 350° oven 1¾ hours. Remove from oven. Take off the lid and weigh the pâté down with a heavy plate and can of tuna until cool. Refrigerate for 24 to 48 hours before serving.

LANGUEDOC PÂTÉS

Languedoc is the last wilderness in France. A legend tells us the giant Gargantua carved out its deep canyons. And, we know the earliest inhabitants were the Cro-Magnons, who settled in the many caves of the Lozère and Périgord; their paintings still survive. Since that time, many others have passed that way, including the Visigoths and Romans. Languedoc was also the home of the Wild Beast of

Gévaudan, who terrorized the countryside from 1764 to 1767. Today, this desolate area is still thought to be haunted by demons and witches. Sheep graze on these lonely plateaus guarded by the dark silhouettes of hooded and caped shepherds. Languedocians are austere men and women of few words, but once they accept you you can count on their life-long friendship. Their cuisine consists of hearty, lusty foods and their pâtés are dark and spiced, full of peppercorns and herbs. The wines come from wild, windblown, gnarled little vines and the end result is heady. Roquefort cheese is produced in this region. Here, we give you pâtés specialties from Cevenol.

PÂTÉ DE LA VIEILLE VICTOIRE

PREPARATION:

45 minutes (marinate overnight)

COOKING TIME:

1 hour at 400° and ½ hour at 350°

INGREDIENTS:

Marinade:
  2 cups dry white wine
⅓ cup brandy
½ teaspoon salt
½ teaspoon freshly ground black pepper
¼ teaspoon allspice

1 bay or laurel leaf
1 teaspoon thyme
4 whole cloves

1 2- to 3-pound rabbit
1 pound pork sausage, ground
2 slices Canadian bacon, finely chopped
½ teaspoon salt
¼ teaspoon freshly ground black pepper
  Pinch of allspice
3 shallots
2 cloves garlic
3 tablespoons chopped parsley
1 large egg, lightly beaten
4 tablespoons + 1½ cups reserved marinade (see above)
1 thin piece lace fat, approximately 14″ x 14″
1 thin (⅛″) piece back fat, approximately 6″x 6″
  Crisco or other shortening
1 large yellow onion, cut in quarters
3 slices carrot
¼ teaspoon salt
⅛ teaspoon freshly ground black pepper
1 bay or laurel leaf

MAKES:

1 medium terrine (1½ quarts) or Pyrex loaf pan (8½ x 4½ x 2½).

METHOD:

Combine the marinade ingredients in a large bowl. Remove the meat from the bones of the rabbit and cut it into large pieces. Add the pieces of rabbit meat to the marinade and marinate overnight. The next day, place the ground sausage and finely chopped Canadian bacon into a bowl and add the salt, pepper, and allspice. Finely chop (or process) the shallots, garlic, and parsley and add to the sausage and bacon base. Add the egg and 4 tablespoons of the marinade. Mix well. Remove the rabbit pieces from the marinade and dry well with paper towels. Make sure the piece of lace fat is also dry and lay it over the base of a large, shallow casserole or baking pan which you have greased well. Cut the piece of back fat into finger-length strips. Sprinkle half of the back fat pieces over the piece of lace fat, then half of the rabbit pieces. Spread half the base meat mixture over the rabbit pieces. Then, sprinkle with more back fat pieces, the rest of the rabbit meat, the rest of the back fat, and finish up with the last half of the base meat. When you have finished layering the meats and fats, roll up the pâté mixture in the lace fat as you would a long package (see illustration). Tie the ends and several other places along the length with string. Grease the casserole or baking pan well with Crisco, placing a few pieces of the shortening right under the pâté bundle. Surround the pâté with the quartered onion, the carrot slices, salt, pepper, laurel leaf, and 1½ cups of the marinade. Bake in a preheated 400° oven 1 hour, then lower the oven to 350° and bake ½ hour more. The pâté should be a beautiful brown color. As it cooks, check the level of the liquid, making sure that it does not reduce completely. Add a little wine or marinade, if necessary. When cooked, remove the pâté from the oven and cut and remove the strings. Place the pâté in a fairly close-fitting terrine or casserole, or preferably a 1½-quart Pyrex loaf pan. Allow the pâté to cool, then if you wish to preserve it for 2 to 3 weeks, melt lard in a small pan and pour it over the pâté. This makes an excellent preservative. Chill until ready to slice. This pâté is one of our favorites!

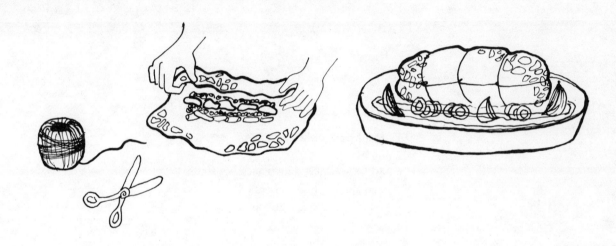

LIVER PÂTÉ CAMPAGNE

PREPARATION:

15 minutes

COOKING TIME:

1½ hours at 350°

INGREDIENTS:

¼ pound pork or beef liver
½ pound pork fat
¼ pound lean pork loin, coarsely ground
1 large shallot, finely chopped
1 garlic clove, finely chopped
1 teaspoon salt
½ teaspoon freshly ground black pepper
  Pinch of allspice
½ teaspoon thyme
2 tablespoons brandy
2 tablespoons dry white wine
1 laurel or bay leaf
1 thin piece lace fat, large enough to line your loaf pan

MAKES:

1 tiny aluminum loaf pan (6 x 3½ x 2)

METHOD:

Clean the pork or beef liver of all fibrous membranes. Have your butcher coarsely grind all the meats (pork liver, pork fat, and fillet of pork) or do it yourself with a Cuisinart or other processor. Place the meat in a mixing bowl. Finely chop or process the shallot and garlic. Add ¾ teaspoon salt, ¼ teaspoon pepper, allspice, ¼ teaspoon thyme, brandy, and white wine, and mix well. Line your terrine or small aluminum pan with the lace fat, draping it way over the sides. Add the pâté mixture, pushing it down so that it is nice and firm. Sprinkle the remaining salt, pepper, and thyme across the top of the pâté. Place the laurel leaf across the center for decoration. Pull up the hanging pieces of lace fat to cover the top completely. Cover with aluminum foil and place the loaf pan in a hot water bath in a medium rectangular pan. Bake in a preheated 350° oven 1½ hours. Remove and weigh the pâté down until cool with a heavy plate and can of tuna. Then refrigerate; when completely cold you can freeze it, if you wish.

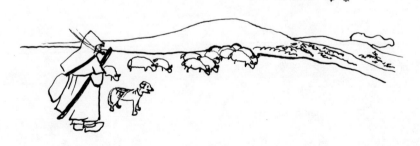

CÔTE d'AZUR

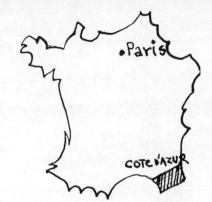

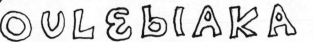

KOULEBIAKA

Koulebiaka is the Russian version of the English pasty and French pâté en croûte. Right after World War I, Nice became a Mecca for White Russian émigrés fleeing the Revolution. Its warm, sunny climate was reminiscent of their Black Sea resorts so popular under the Czar. The little colony quickly made the best of their lot, and it was not uncommon in those days to have an ex-general as your taxi driver, or a poor but noble duchess for a chambermaid. The émigrés, however, added great color and flavor to the cuisine of Nice. Easter time was the favorite festival season and the Russian Orthodox Church blazed with candles as everyone gathered to celebrate the holiday. Elaborate and beautifully decorated eggs were offered for sale and every menu boasted the traditional Koulebiaka. These succulent Russian creations with French overtones, deserve an honored place in anyone's collection. The following delicious fish koulebiaka has been simplified by a wonderful half-French, half-Russian lady chef living in Nice, France.

FISH KOULEBIAKA

PREPARATION:

1 hour

COOKING TIME:

15 minutes at 400° and 45 minutes at 350°

INGREDIENTS:

Dough:
 2 cups all-purpose flour
 ½ pound unsalted butter
 1 teaspoon salt
 ½ cup cold water or more

Pâté Filling:
 2 large eggs, hard cooked and chopped
 ⅔ cup long-grain rice
 1½ cups sour cream
 1½ pounds fresh or frozen salmon (4 thick slices)
 ½ teaspoon salt
 ¼ teaspoon freshly ground black pepper
 1 large egg yolk combined with a little water

½ cup chopped fresh parsley
½ cup chopped fresh dill weed or 2 tablespoons dried dill weed
   Lettuce leaves or other garnish
4 tablespoons butter, melted

MAKES:

6 to 8 slices as a first course, 6 as a luncheon

METHOD:

Dough:
Combine the flour, butter and salt in a bowl until crumbly (we use our fingers).
Add nearly all the water and mix. Add more water if needed. Do not overwork the
dough. As soon as it forms a ball, even if it is not a smooth ball, stop and let it
rest for 30 minutes on a lightly floured breadboard. Then roll it out to make a 12-
inch square. Fold the square in thirds, sides toward the center, overlapping each
other. Let the dough rest 10 minutes more under a well-floured dish towel. Roll it
again to a 12-inch square, fold it in thirds again, then cover with a floured towel
until ready to use.

Pâté Filling:
Coarsely chop the hard-boiled eggs. Cook the rice until *very* tender. Drain the rice
in a colander and run cold water over it. Allow to dry out a bit. Skin and bone the
salmon slices. Roll out your dough into a rectangular shape about ¼ inch thick.
With your rolling pin make the outside edge thinner than the center. Down the

center, make a bed using half the cooked rice. Cover with half the sour cream and place the salmon slices over the cream. Season with salt and pepper (add a bit more pepper than salt). Cover with the remaining sour cream. Finally sprinkle the chopped egg over all, salt and pepper it and top with ¼ cup of the chopped parsley and ¼ cup of the chopped fresh dill (or 1 tablespoon dried). Wet the edges of pastry with a brush or your finger dipped in water and fold into a rectangular package, with double layers of dough on the top. Slide package onto a piece of waxed paper so you can then turn it over onto an aluminum-foil-covered cookie sheet. After you have turned the package over, the double layers of dough will now be on the bottom and will seal together as the Koulebiaka bakes. The single layer

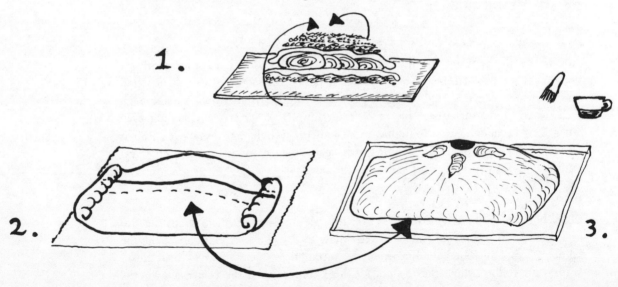

of dough will now be on top. Brush with the egg yolk and water. Cut a hole in the center about the size of a quarter and also prick the top four or five times with a fork. Place in a preheated 400° oven 15 minutes. As soon as the top starts to brown (a nice golden brown), lower heat to 350° and bake 45 minutes longer. Remove when the Koulebiaka is well browned.

Place on a serving dish surrounded by lettuce or whatever decoration inspires you most. Just before serving combine the melted butter with the remaining parsley and dill (¼ cup each) and pour this into the quarter-size hole on the top of the Koulebiaka.

VEAL KOULEBIAKA

PREPARATION:

1 hour

COOKING TIME:

45 minutes at 350°

INGREDIENTS:

Dough:
  2 cups all-purpose flour
 ½ pound unsalted butter
  1 teaspoon salt
 ½ cup cold water or more

Pâté Filling:
½ pound veal, ground
 4 tablespoons butter
 2 large eggs, hard cooked
 1 pound green cabbage
½ pound bacon
 1 tablespoon chopped parsley
 1 teaspoon chopped dill weed

½ teaspoon salt
½ teaspoon freshly ground black pepper
1 large egg yolk combined with a little water

MAKES:

4 slices

METHOD:

Dough:

Combine the flour, butter and salt together in a bowl until crumbly (we use our fingers). Add nearly all the water and mix. Add more water if needed. Do not overwork the dough. As soon as it forms a ball, even if it is not a smooth ball, stop and let it rest for 30 minutes on a lightly floured breadboard. Then roll it out to make a 12-inch square. Fold the square in thirds, sides toward the center overlapping each other. Let the dough rest 10 minutes more under a well floured dish towel. Roll it again to a 12-inch square, fold it in thirds again then cover with a floured towel until ready to use.

Pâté Filling:

Sauté the ground veal in 2 tablespoons butter and let it cool. Chop the eggs. Blanch the cabbage in boiling water for a few moments, and chop it fine. Chop the bacon fine. Mix with the cabbage. Roll out the Koulebiaka dough into a rectangle. Place a layer of cabbage and bacon mixture on the bottom. On top of that put a layer of sautéed ground veal, then another of chopped cabbage and finally a layer of chopped egg, parsley, salt, dill, and pepper. Roll it up as for Fish Koulebiaka (page 62). Cut a hole in the top. Brush with the egg yolk and water. Place on a greased piece of aluminum foil on a cookie sheet and bake in a preheated 350° oven 30 to 40 minutes or until well browned. Melt 2 tablespoons of butter and pour into the hole on top just before serving.

RABBIT IN ASPIC

PREPARATION:

1 hour

COOKING TIME:

1 hour at 350°

INGREDIENTS:

1 2-pound rabbit, with liver and kidneys

Court Bouillon:
    Rabbit bones
    Water to cover
1 large yellow onion, cut in quarters

3 carrots, sliced
1 teaspoon salt
  A few whole black peppercorns
1 whole clove garlic

2 tablespoons dry white wine
⅛ teaspoon freshly ground black pepper
½ teaspoon salt
1 tablespoon finely chopped parsley
1 tablespoon finely chopped chives
  Pinch of chervil
½ envelope unflavored gelatin

MAKES:

1 small terrine (3 cups)

METHOD:

Remove the rabbit meat from the bones. Make the court bouillon by placing the rabbit bones in a large pot, adding water to cover and adding the onion, carrots, salt, peppercorns, and garlic. Simmer one hour without a lid and strain, reserving about 1½ cups liquid.

Place the rabbit meat, liver and kidneys in a 1½-quart terrine or loaf pan (you will transfer into a smaller terrine after the rabbit is baked). Add the white wine and enough court bouillon to cover entirely. Add the pepper, salt, parsley, chives,

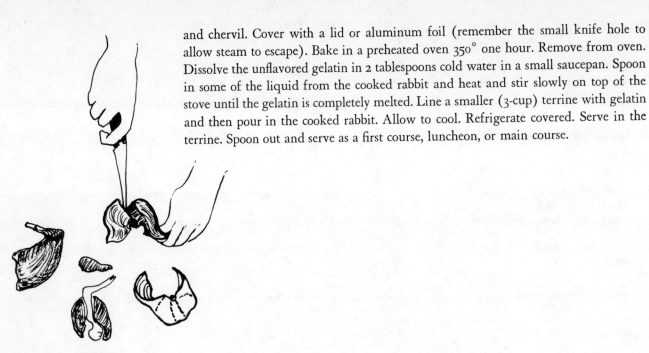

and chervil. Cover with a lid or aluminum foil (remember the small knife hole to allow steam to escape). Bake in a preheated oven 350° one hour. Remove from oven. Dissolve the unflavored gelatin in 2 tablespoons cold water in a small saucepan. Spoon in some of the liquid from the cooked rabbit and heat and stir slowly on top of the stove until the gelatin is completely melted. Line a smaller (3-cup) terrine with gelatin and then pour in the cooked rabbit. Allow to cool. Refrigerate covered. Serve in the terrine. Spoon out and serve as a first course, luncheon, or main course.

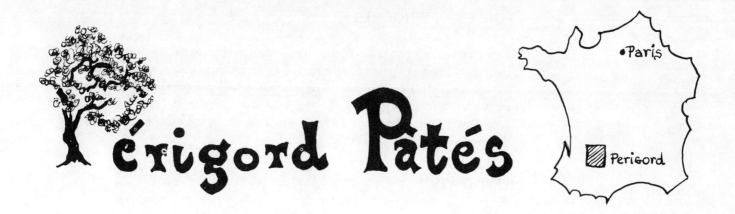

Périgord Pátés

The truffle, with its haunting odor of primeval forest, is known as the "black diamond of the Périgord." We prefer Colette's description, "the most venerated of black Princesses!"

Surely no other ingredient has done more for pâté than Périgord's subterranean treasure. Unfortunately, *la truffe* is now a rare luxury. During the 1900s, 130 tons of truffles were produced in Périgord and today a mere 10 tons! Men have tried to grow them elsewhere with very little success, because it is impossible to duplicate the Périgord soil, its climate, its pubescent oak trees, and the crafty Perigourdins with their magic dogs and pigs.

Once in a while, however, everyone should splurge on a small can of truffles or truffle peelings. Truffles have a very subtle way of pepping up any pâté and making it something very special.

FOIE GRAS BRIOCHES

In France, fresh foie gras (goose liver) can be purchased as whole two-pound individual livers. The geese are force-fed to create these enlarged livers, which are buttery rich when cooked and from which the fabled Foie Gras Pâté industry of France has sprung. In the United States, such livers are simply not available. Instead, order goose livers from your meat or poultry man in the amount required. Shops that stock live poultry usually have them.

PREPARATION:

1 hour

COOKING TIME:

15 minutes to bake the livers at 250°
20 to 25 minutes at 375° for the brioches

INGREDIENTS:

Cuisinart Brioche Dough:
  1 envelope active dry yeast
  ¼ cup lukewarm milk
     Pinch + ¼ cup sugar
2¼ cups sifted all-purpose flour
  3 large eggs, lightly beaten

¾ teaspoon salt
¾ cup unsalted butter, softened

10 goose livers (about 2 pounds)
1 truffle
3 tablespoons Armagnac
1 thin piece of lace fat, to encase the livers
1 large egg yolk, lightly beaten

MAKES:

10 brioches

METHOD:

Cuisinart Brioche Dough:
Prepare brioche dough one day in advance. In a bowl, soften the yeast in the luke-warm milk along with the sugar for 10 minutes. Add ½ cup sifted flour and stir the yeast and flour just until mixed. Cut a deep **X** in the mixture and sift one cup flour over it and, without combining, let the yeast mixture rise, covered with a tea towel, in a warm place for one hour. In the Cuisinart unit, using the steel **S**-shaped blade, combine the rising yeast flour, ¼ cup sugar, the eggs and salt. Turn the machine on and mix 2½ minutes. Spread the softened butter over the dough in the machine and turn on for a few more seconds, just until the butter is mixed through. Put the dough on a lightly floured surface and using your fingers, knead in about ¾ cup more sifted flour. Place the dough in a buttered bowl and let it rise, covered,

for 3 hours or until it is three times its original size. Punch down the dough, put it in another bowl, cover with plastic wrap and a dish towel and chill overnight.

Clean and gently pare the goose livers. Try to retain their original shapes without mashing them. Slice the truffle in very thin slices and soak briefly in Armagnac just to cover (about 1 tablespoon). Make small knife slits in each liver and insert a thin slice of truffle in each one. Place in a bowl and pour the truffle marinade plus two more tablespoons of Armagnac over the livers and let them soak for 30 minutes. Remove and pat dry. Wrap each liver in a piece of lace fat or several very thin pieces of back fat (never use bacon) and place in a pie pan or baking dish. Place in a 250° oven for 15 minutes. Let cool slightly and remove the lace fat.

Punch down the brioche dough and divide into 10 balls. Make sure your hands are floured for this process. Using two-thirds of each ball, mold the dough into the holes of a brioche pan or muffin tin. Make a cavity in the center and place one goose liver in each. Cover each cavity with the remaining ⅓ of each ball for a top crust. Let the stuffed brioche dough rise again one last time in a warm place for about 3 hours. Brush the top of each brioche with egg yolk and place the tins on a cookie sheet in a preheated 375° oven 15 to 20 minutes or until brown. Remove and serve immediately.

WHOLE CHICKEN LIVER PÂTÉ WITH TRUFFLE PEELINGS

PREPARATION:

30 minutes

COOKING TIME:

1 hour at 350°

INGREDIENTS:

½ pound firm chicken livers, left whole
1 1-ounce can truffle peelings, with juice reserved
4 tablespoons port
2 tablespoons whiskey
½ pound chicken hearts (if unobtainable use chicken livers)
¼ pound pork fat, ground
½ pound lean pork, ground
¼ pound bacon, ground
½ teaspoon salt
½ teaspoon freshly ground black pepper
   Pinch of allspice
1 thin piece lace fat

MAKES:

1 medium terrine (1½ quarts) or 1 aluminum loaf pan (8½ x 4½ x 2½) plus 1 small
loaf pan (6 x 3½ x 2)

METHOD:

Clean and trim the chicken livers. Marinate the livers and truffle peelings for 2 hours in the port, whiskey, and truffle juice. To make the base, grind up the hearts, pork fat, lean pork and bacon in a Cuisinart or other processor. Place in a bowl and add the salt, pepper and allspice. Mix thoroughly. Drain the livers and add the marinade to the base meats. Place the lace fat in the terrine or loaf pans, draping it over the sides. Put on a layer of the base, a layer of chicken livers, a layer of the base, then chicken livers, ending with a layer of the base. Salt and pepper very lightly between the layers. Pull up the draped lace fat and cover with its lid or aluminum foil. Punch a hole in the foil to let the steam escape. Place in hot water bath in a large rectangular pan and bake in a preheated 350° oven one hour. Remove from oven and weigh down with a heavy plate and can of tuna until cool. Refrigerate for 24 hours before serving.

FOIE GRAS EN CROÛTE

PREPARATION:

1 hour

COOKING TIME:

1 hour at 400°

INGREDIENTS:

Dough:
 2 cups all-purpose flour
½ pound unsalted butter
 1 teaspoon salt
½ cup cold water or more

 1 7-ounce can foie gras
 1 large egg yolk, lightly beaten with a little water

MAKES:

1 tiny aluminum loaf pan (6 x 3½ x 2)

METHOD:

Dough:

Make your dough several hours in advance. Mix flour, salt and butter together in a bowl until crumbly (we use our fingers). Add nearly all the water and mix. Add more water if needed. Do not overwork the dough. As soon as it forms a ball, even if it is not a smooth ball, stop and let it rest for 30 minutes on a lightly floured breadboard. Then roll it out to make a 12-inch square. Fold the square in thirds, sides toward the center overlapping each other. Let the dough rest 10 minutes more under a well floured dish towel. Roll it again to a 12-inch square, fold it in thirds again, then cover with a floured towel until ready to use.

Roll out two thirds of the dough to about ⅛ inch thick or a little thinner and line an appropriate baking dish with the dough, overlapping the edges about one inch. Use a dish or pan that provides a fairly snug fit for the shape of the foie gras you bought. Open the tin and place the block of formed foie gras on top of the dough in the baking dish. Brush the edges with a little of the egg yolk and water. Roll out the remaining third of dough and lay across the top. Press the edges together firmly, turning them under on the inside of the baking dish to form a nice block effect when baked. Cut a small hole in the center to allow steam to escape, and brush with more egg yolk mixture. You can decorate the top of the dough before you bake it by cutting out leaf shapes and sticking them on with a little egg yolk. Bake in a preheated 400° oven one hour. The dough should be well browned and attractive. Cool and serve at room temperature or chilled. This is a very quick and easy pâté en croûte.

Basque Pâtés

Paris

Pays Basque

The deep mountain passes and valleys in the Basque country made possible a very curious hunt which dates far back in the nebulous Basque history. Legend tells us that Sanche VII, the seventeenth Basque king of the Arizta dynasty, installed the first dove nets high on top of the Lepheder Pass in the Pyrenees Mountains between France and Spain. In 1237, King Charles II ordered posts to be driven into the ground so that the incredibly tall wooden watchtowers could be build for dove hunting. Today only seven or eight of these towers remain.

In spite of modern shotguns and shells, the Basques still climb their watchtowers every October, waiting and watching for the dove migration from North Africa, across Spain, to their country. Nets are stretched across the mouths of the valleys and after days of vigil a great shout rings from tower to tower and white flags are waved as the watchers announce the arrival of the birds. Then men with centuries of jai alai in their blood hurl platelike stones at the lead birds, causing them to swoop low and into the nets. Originally, a sport of kings!

We include a recipe for dove pie (we usually make it with squab).

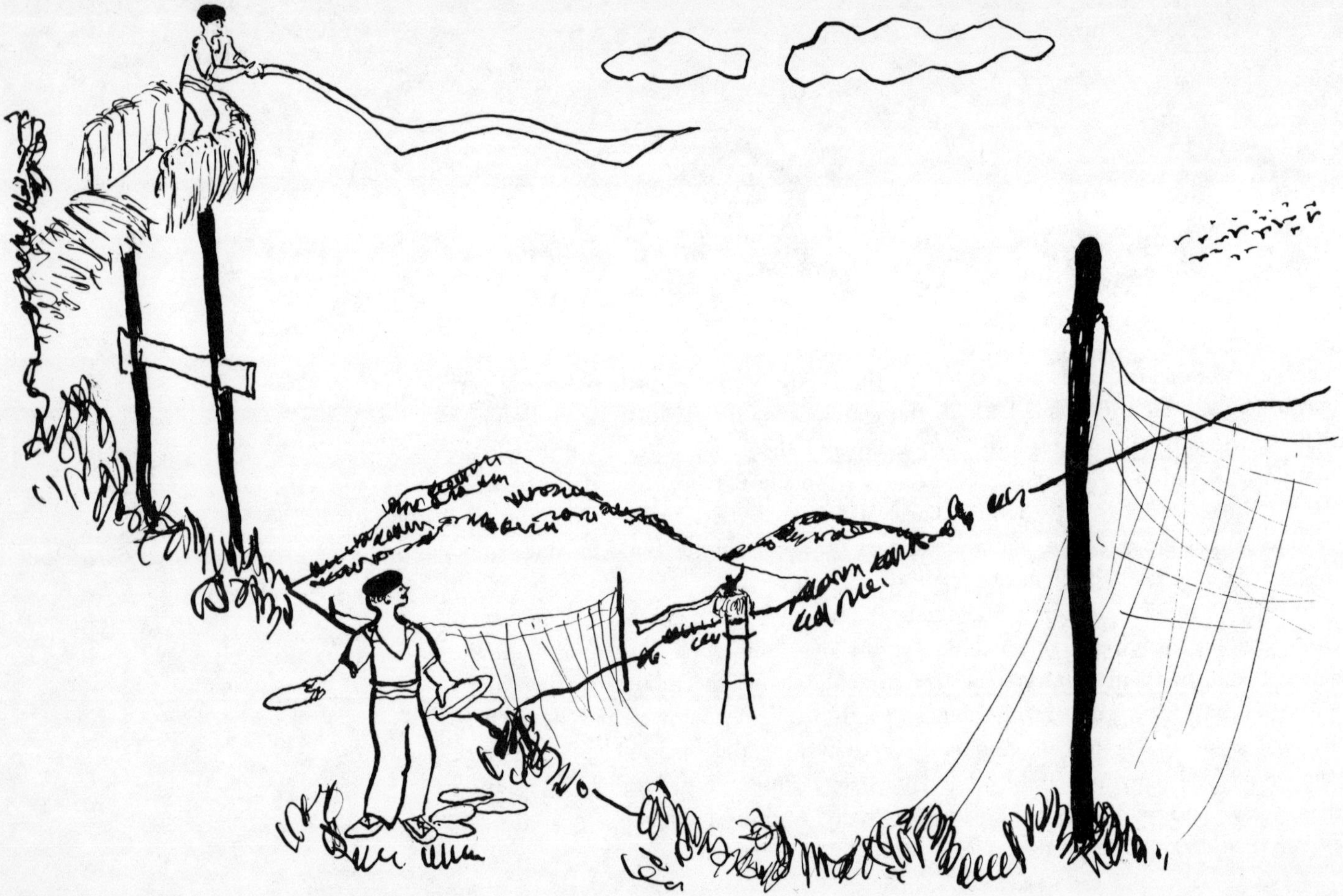

BASQUE DOVE TORTE

PREPARATION:

30 minutes (make the dough 1 hour in advance)

COOKING TIME:

1 hour at 350°

INGREDIENTS:

Dough:
  1 cup all-purpose flour
  ¼ pound unsalted butter
  ½ teaspoon salt
  ¼ cup cold water or more

  1 tablespoon margarine
  2 tablespoons vegetable oil
  2 squab, with gizzards and livers reserved
  4 tablespoons butter
  1 ¼-pound slab of bacon, cubed
15 small white onions
  ½ pound mushrooms, sliced
  ½ pound chicken livers, cleaned and trimmed

1½ tablespoons brandy
1½ tablespoons Madeira
¼ teaspoon salt
¼ teaspoon freshly ground black pepper
⅛ teaspoon sage (scant)
   A good pinch of thyme
½ tablespoon flour
 1 large egg yolk, lightly beaten with water

MAKES:

One 9- or 10-inch pie or an 8 x 8-inch square Pyrex baking dish

METHOD:

Dough:

Make dough several hours in advance. Mix flour, salt and butter together in a bowl until crumbly (we use our fingers). Add nearly all the water and mix. Add more water if needed. Do not overwork the dough. As soon as it forms a ball, even if it is not a smooth ball, stop and let it rest for 30 minutes on a lightly floured bread-board. Then roll it out to make a 12-inch square. Fold the square in thirds, sides toward the center overlapping each other. Let the dough rest 10 minutes more under a well-floured dish towel. Roll it again to a 12-inch square, fold it in thirds again, then cover with floured towel until ready to use.

   Melt the margarine and oil in a deep casserole pot on top of the stove over medium heat. Add the two whole squab and sauté until brown. Remove the squab and pour out the margarine and oil. Wipe the pot out with paper towels. This is important and makes a great taste difference in the final dish. In the same pot, melt the butter over medium heat and add the bacon cubes and the small white onions (frozen are fine) and sauté until golden. Quarter the squab and place on a large plate. Remove the bacon and onions and place over the top of the squab pieces. Be sure there is enough butter left in the pot to sauté the mushrooms. If not, add one tablespoon butter and brown them. Remove the mushrooms with a slotted spoon and place on top of the bacon and onions. Place the gizzards and livers of the squab plus the chicken livers in the pot and sauté just until firm. Remove from the pan and place on top of the mushrooms. To the juices left in the pan, add the brandy, Madeira, salt, pepper, sage, and thyme. Stir to a quick boil, getting up all the particles left in the pot, stir in ½ tablespoon flour to thicken, and remove from the flame. Put all the sautéed ingredients you have previously layered on the plate into a pie plate or square Pyrex dish. Pour over the brandy and Madeira sauce.

Roll out the dough you made earlier in the day to a larger size than your dish. Cut four strips if your dish is square, or several strips to overlap if your dish is round, and place them along the edges of your dish. Brush them with the egg yolk and water and lay the rest of the dough over the pie, touching these strips and forming a seal as you press them together. Brush the top with the egg yolk. Prick the top four or five times with a knife to allow steam to escape. Bake in a preheated 350° oven one hour or until well browned. Remove and slice at the table.

RABBIT AND GREEN OLIVE PÂTÉ

PREPARATION:

1 hour

COOKING TIME:

1¾ hours at 350°

INGREDIENTS:

1 3½-pound rabbit, with liver reserved
1 pound lean veal
10 ounces pork fat
10 ounces lean pork
1 tablespoon salt
1 teaspoon freshly ground black pepper
1 teaspoon thyme
¼ teaspoon allspice
1 laurel or bay leaf
8 ounces pimiento-stuffed green olives
⅓ cup brandy
⅔ cup dry white wine
1 thin piece lace fat, large enough to line the terrine
   Pitted stuffed green olives, sliced, as garnish

MAKES:

1 2-quart rectangular cast iron pâté terrine

METHOD:

Buy a 3½-pound rabbit and have your butcher cut off the two hind quarters and two front quarters, leaving the middle whole. Use your sharpest small kitchen knife and pare the meat off each piece of rabbit. The filets of the rabbit comes from the middle piece. Cut these carefully and reserve these choice pieces. Put the rest of the rabbit meat along with its liver, half the lean pork, a third of the veal, and all the pork fat through a Cuisinart or other processor, medium grind. In one bowl put the filets of the rabbit and the rest of the lean pork and veal, which has been sliced into finger-length pieces. Pour over the brandy and white wine and marinate for a little while. In another bowl put the ground meats and add the salt, pepper, thyme, and allspice and mix well. Remove the pimientos from the green olives and set aside. Chop the olives and set aside. Pour off the marinade and add to the ground meat mixture. Reserve the filets of rabbit, veal and pork. Line the terrine with the lace fat, draping it over the sides. Put first a layer of half the base meat. Then sprinkle in a layer of half the chopped olives. Layer all the large pieces of rabbit, veal, and pork in the center. Sprinkle with the pimientos. Add the last layer of chopped green olives and finish with the rest of your base meat layered on top. Sprinkle pepper over the top generously as rabbit is a bit bland, and sprinkle some salt over all. Place the laurel leaf in the center for decoration and pull up the sides of the lace fat overhanging the terrine. Cover the top of the pâté with the lid or aluminum foil. If using foil, punch a hole to let the steam escape. Set your terrine in a hot water bath in a large rectangular pan. Bake in a preheated 350° oven 1¾ hours. After the terrine is baked, remove and weigh the pâté down with a heavy plate and can of tuna until cool and then refrigerate 24 hours before serving. Decorate with slices of stuffed green olives.

Breton Pâtés

Brittany is a region of druids, of Merlin the Magician and his forest, and of azalea-covered castles which inspired the fairy tales of Sleeping Beauty and Cinderella. Originally a very poor province, it is only in recent years that the Breton peasant has acquired a little wealth with the influx of the Parisian tourists. Its coastline produces an abundance of delicious fish and its peasant cuisine is famous for its charcuterie. Even today the Breton usually has but a few cows and one or two pigs. He has to transform the latter into every appetizing dish imaginable. He does very well indeed. You can feast on andouille and andouillette (smoked sausages made from mysterious parts of the pig). The Breton pâté in particular has an aromatic liver flavor all its own, due to the Breton's imaginative use of pork liver, heart and melt—a great triumvirate!

PÂTÉ BRETON

PREPARATION:

35 minutes, plus refrigeration overnight

COOKING TIME:

45 minutes at 400° and 1¼ hours at 350°

INGREDIENTS:

¾ pound pork liver, coarsely chopped
¾ pound lean shoulder of pork, ground
1 pound 5 ounces white pork fat (without a trace of meat), ground
2 ounces veal heart, finely chopped
2 ounces pork melt, chopped medium
2¼ tablespoons salt
1½ teaspoons freshly ground black pepper
2 tablespoons brandy
½ teaspoon thyme
1½ medium yellow onions, finely chopped
1 thin piece of lace fat, large enough to line your terrines and drape over sides

MAKES:

2 medium terrines (1½ quarts) or 2 disposable aluminum loaf pans (8½ x 4½ x 2)

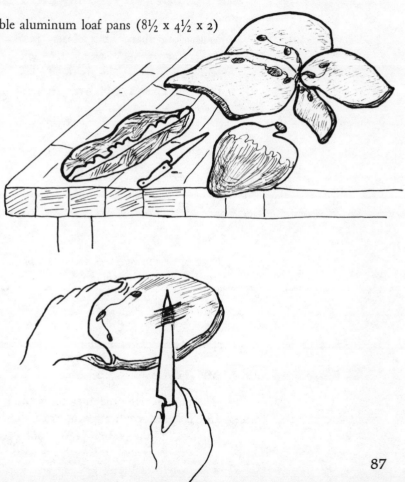

Heart, liver, and melt of the pork

Insert knife into piece of liver, just barely under the skin, lift up and pull away paper-thin membrane. Repeat all around outside of liver.

With your sharp knife, insert just under fat on one side of the melt and pull away easily all the fat of the melt. Then, as with liver, remove membrane.

Slice open the heart and render the inside completely smooth.

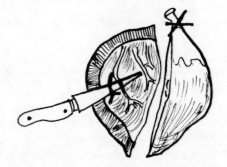

METHOD:

Thoroughly trim the membrane and veins from the pork liver and veal heart. In Cuisinart or other processor coarsely chop the liver. Finely chop heart, melt, and onions. Add the ground pork shoulder and pork fat and thoroughly mix together in a large bowl. Add the salt, pepper, and brandy. Mix again. Cover with plastic wrap and refrigerate overnight to marry the flavors. When ready to bake, line the terrines or loaf pans with the lace fat, draping it one to two inches over the sides. Fill the pans with the pâté, and sprinkle with salt, pepper, and the thyme. Fold the lace fat over the top and press down to make a compact mass. Place terrines or loaf pans in hot water baths in large rectangular pans. Bake in a preheated 400° oven 45 minutes, then lower the heat to 350° and continue baking 1¼ hours. The lace fat should brown. Your pâtés are done if the fat surrounding them in the pans is clear. Remove from oven and weigh down with a heavy plate and can of tuna. When completely cool, refrigerate 24 hours, covered, to allow the pâté to settle before serving. This chunky, hearty country pâté will keep beautifully for two weeks in the refrigerator.

ARTICHOKE AND HAM PÂTÉ

PREPARATION:

20 minutes

COOKING TIME:

45 minutes at 350° for a soufflé dish
30 minutes at 350° in individual ramekins or until slightly puffed and brown

INGREDIENTS:

4 large artichokes
2 large eggs, separated
3 tablespoons heavy cream
½ teaspoon salt
¼ teaspoon freshly ground black pepper
¼ cup minced cooked ham
2 teaspoons finely chopped shallots
2 tablespoons grated Swiss cheese

Béchamel Sauce:
2 tablespoons butter
1½ to 2 tablespoons all-purpose flour
1 cup milk
Salt and freshly ground black pepper to taste

MAKES:

1 medium soufflé dish (1 quart) or 6 4-ounce ramekins

METHOD:

Boil the artichokes until well done. Remove or eat the leaves. Clean away the choke from the bottoms and purée the bottoms in a Cuisinart or other processor. Place this mixture into a bowl and add the egg yolks, heavy cream, salt, pepper, ham, and finely minced shallots. Mix thoroughly. Beat the egg whites until stiff and fold into the artichoke mixture carefully. Spoon into a soufflé dish or individual ramkins and sprinkle the grated Swiss cheese over the top. Bake in a preheated 350° oven 45 minutes, if in a soufflé dish, or 30 minutes if in ramekins.

Béchamel Sauce:
Melt the butter in a saucepan slowly. Add the flour and stir with a wire whisk or wooden spoon until well blended. Stir in the milk very slowly, stirring constantly to prevent lumps. Add salt and pepper to taste.

Check the pâté to see if it is nicely browned and slightly puffed; if not, leave in a little longer. Spoon some Béchamel Sauce on top and serve the remaining Sauce in a separate bowl.

NORMANDY PÂTÉS

NORMANDY

• paris

BAYEUX TAPESTRY

The Normandy coast "off season" is a luxury in which few people are interested. Perhaps it is the rain (making Normandy so green) that visitors dislike or the enormous, empty fin de siècle villas that line the coast, a stark contrast with the lovely Norman manor houses and farms of the interior. Once, we were lent one of the monstrous villas but we found something nostalgically attractive about it, right down to its enormous glazed tile roof on which sat a porcelain rabbit and cat. We were always wondering about what it must have been like in its heyday.

Perhaps the most relaxing thing that ever happened to the present owners of this villa was to arrive from Paris one weekend and be received by us in their own home. We had been shopping that morning in the delightful fifteenth-century *halle* (covered marketplace) in nearby Dives-sur-Mer. We bought three or four pâtés, a Camembert just on the verge of abandoning itself, beautiful *pissenlits* (dandelions) for a salad full of crisp pieces of bacon, and finally a great bowl of fromage blanc with several ladles of thick Norman crème fraîche on the side. So much for food! Drink came in the form of Norman cider . . . *et voilà*. Our time preparing the luncheon was effortless and the guests ate with such gusto that an afternoon's nap was barely enough to revive them. We awakened in time for a long walk along the seashore, and unfortunately, all this did was to work up a ravenous appetite for yet another enormous meal.

CHICKEN LIVER GATEAU À LA NORMANDE

PREPARATION:

14 minutes

COOKING TIME:

45 minutes at 350°

INGREDIENTS:

 8 chicken livers
½ cup all-purpose flour
 5 large eggs
 3 large egg yolks
 1 pint heavy cream
   Pinch of cloves
 1 tablespoon salt
 1 teaspoon freshly ground white pepper

2 teaspoons chopped parsley
1 clove garlic, crushed

Tomato Sauce:
4 large ripe tomatoes, peeled
1 large yellow onion, finely chopped
2 tablespoons butter
¼ teaspoon salt
¼ teaspoon freshly ground black pepper
2 teaspoons parsley, minced
½ teaspoon sugar
3 tablespoons tomato paste

MAKES:

12 4-ounce ramekins or 2 medium baking dishes (1 quart)

METHOD:

Clean and pare the chicken livers. Chop finely or grind them in a Cuisinart or other processor. Combine the flour, eggs, egg yolks, cream, cloves, salt, pepper, parsley, and garlic together thoroughly. Mix in the chopped chicken livers and pour into buttered ramekins about ¾ full. Place the ramekins in a hot water bath in a large rectangular pan and bake in a preheated oven at 350° about 45 minutes.

Tomato Sauce:

Peel the tomatoes and chop. Chop the onions very finely and sauté in the butter until golden. Add the tomatoes, salt, pepper, parsley and sugar. Simmer 45 minutes. Add the tomato paste, and stir through to heat.

Test with a knife about 35 minutes into the baking of the chicken liver cakes to see if it comes out clean. Remove from the oven and hot water bath. Unmold and serve hot, or chill and then unmold and serve cold. Spoon the Tomato Sauce over the top of each ramekin. These chicken liver cakes make a delicious and delicate first course or luncheon.

MOUSSE OF CHICKEN LIVERS DIVOISE

PREPARATION:

15 minutes

COOKING TIME:

40 minutes at 350°

INGREDIENTS:

½ pound chicken livers
1 tablespoon butter

¾ cup heavy cream
2 large eggs
½ teaspoon nutmeg (scant)
½ teaspoon salt
½ teaspoon freshly ground black pepper

MAKES:

6 4-ounce ramekins

METHOD:

Clean and trim the chicken livers, removing any dark spots. Sauté the livers in the butter. Purée them in the Cuisinart or other processor. Pour into a bowl and add the heavy cream and eggs. Add the nutmeg, salt, and pepper. The mixture should have the consistency of thick cream. Pour into little buttered ovenproof ramekins or dishes and put in a water bath on top of the stove. Cook gently about 25 minutes. Then place the ovenproof dishes in their water bath and bake in a preheated 350° oven 15 minutes. This pâté is one of the most delicate. It can be served in small individual ramekins as a first course with thin slices of French bread or as an hors d'oeuvre in a larger dish.

CELERY ROOT PÂTÉ

PREPARATION:

30 minutes

COOKING TIME:

45 minutes at 350°

INGREDIENTS:

  4 small celery roots
¾ cup grated Swiss cheese
½ teaspoon salt
¼ teaspoon freshly ground black pepper
  2 large eggs, separated

Béchamel Sauce:
  2 tablespoons butter
1½ to 2 tablespoons flour
  1 cup milk
    Salt and pepper
  1 tablespoon tomato paste

MAKES:

1 medium soufflé dish (1 quart)

METHOD:

Peel and clean the celery roots and cut them into big chunks. Cook in boiling water until well done. Purée in a Cuisinart or other processor and place in a bowl. Add the grated cheese, salt, pepper, and egg yolks. Mix thoroughly. Beat the egg whites until stiff and fold into the celery root mixture. Butter the soufflé dish and spoon in the mixture. Place in a preheated 350° oven and bake 45 minutes or until the pâté is slightly puffed and firm.

Béchamel Sauce:
Melt buttter in a saucepan, slowly. Add the flour and stir with a wire whisk until well blended. Stir in the milk very slowly, stirring constantly to prevent lumps. Add one tablespoon of tomato paste. The sauce should be a salmon-pink color.

Remove pâté from the oven and turn out on a serving plate. Spoon some of the Béchamel Sauce over the top and serve hot, with the rest of the sauce on the side.

Picardy Pâtés

Picardy is the ideal place for duck and fish. Its vast ponds are spread over thousands of acres in this rich farm area of northern France, fed by the wide Somme river and many smaller streams. Ducks who manage to get this far north follow a centuries-old flight pattern to and from their winter and summer homes. The hunters get into their duck blinds and blast away with special duck *canons* and beautiful retrievers hurl themselves into the icy ponds bringing back teals, mallards and widgeons. Then, it's all up to the mistress of the house to transform them into pâtés. We did this task for an endless number of years, even canning our own. Believe us, it's a wonderful sight to behold a shelf of your very own pâtés. Always leave one from the year before and you will end up with great "years," as with Bordeaux and Burgundies.

We include three pâtés from Picardy. One is the famous Pâté d'Amiens. The celebrated seventeenth-century lady of letters, Madame de Sévigné, after having tasted it, wrote immediately to her daughter telling her that "nothing was comparable to this delicious pâté, with its crust more golden, more blond than the curls of the little Lavardin girl!"

Another pâté is a family standby in the Somme. We made it with enormous pike caught from our ponds, but you can make it just as well with salmon, white fish, or lake bass.

FISH PÂTÉ FROM PICARDY

PREPARATION:

30 minutes

COOKING TIME:

15 minutes at 400° and 45 minutes at 350°

INGREDIENTS

Dough:
 2 cups all-purpose flour

½ pound unsalted butter
1 teaspoon salt
½ cup cold water or more

Court Bouillon:
1 cup dry white wine
1 tablespoon salt
8 peppercorns
1 rib celery
1 laurel or bay leaf
1 small carrot, sliced
½ medium yellow onion, sliced

2 pounds fresh salmon, pike, or perch
8 large white mushroom caps
½ cup butter, softened
1 teaspoon salt
½ teaspoon freshly ground black pepper
¼ teaspoon ground nutmeg
¼ cup heavy cream
¼ teaspoon chervil
1 teaspoon tarragon
4 tablespoons butter
1 large egg yolk, lightly beaten with water

MAKES:

A rectangular pie of 8 slices

METHOD:

Dough:
Mix flour, salt and butter together in a bowl until crumbly (we use our fingers).
Add nearly all the water and mix. Add more water if needed. Do not overwork
the dough. As soon as it forms a ball, even if it is not a smooth ball, stop and let it
rest for 30 minutes on a lightly floured breadboard. Then roll it out to make a 12-
inch square. Fold the square in thirds, sides toward the center overlapping each
other. Let the dough rest 10 minutes more under a well-floured dish towel. Roll it
out again to a 12-inch square, fold it in thirds again then cover with a floured towel
until ready to use.

Court Bouillon:
Place the piece of fish in a deep saucepan with the wine and enough water to cover.
Add the salt, peppercorns, celery, laurel or bay leaf, carrot, and the onion. Poach the
fish in the Court Bouillon until cooked, but still firm, about 10 minutes.

Fish Pâté:
When the fish is poached, chill it slightly to make it easier to cut. Cut the skin
off and then cut the fish in half down the middle of the back. Take one half of the
fish along with the mushroom caps and purée in the food processor or Cuisinart
until the mixture is a compact mass. Put the mixture in a bowl with the softened

butter and mix well with your hands. Add the salt, pepper, nutmeg, and heavy cream. The fish mixture should be the consistency of a very spreadable paste.

Roll out the dough into a rectangle. Spread half the fish paste in the center. Sprinkle a little salt and pepper over the mixture. Cut the other half of the poached fish into finger-length pieces and place them over the paste in a layer. Heat the remaining 4 tablespoons butter in a small saucepan just until melted, and add the chervil and tarragon. Mix together and pour over the fish pieces. Spread the other half of the fish paste over the entire mixture and bring up the two sides of the dough, folding one side over the other. Seal with a little water. Roll up each end and turn over on a foil-covered cookie sheet (17 x 14). Make a hole in the center about the size of a quarter. Brush with the egg yolk mixed with water and bake in a preheated 400° oven for 15 minutes or until golden brown. Lower the oven to 350° and continue baking for 45 minutes more. This pie should be a luscious golden brown. Slice and serve hot. Great for a first course or luncheon, or supper for 2 to 4 guests.

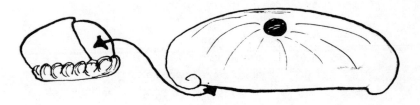

PÂTÉ DE CAMPAGNE G. DUMONT

PREPARATION:

30 minutes and 3 hours for marinating

COOKING TIME:

1½ hours at 350°

INGREDIENTS

9 ounces lean pork
5 ounces white pork fat
3 shallots, chopped
2 cloves garlic, chopped
1 teaspoon salt
1 teaspoon freshly ground black pepper
4 tablespoons brandy
2 tablespoons Madeira
5 ounces lean veal
5 ounces ham
2 large eggs
2 tablespoons chopped parsley
  Thin (⅛″) strips back fat for lining your terrines

MAKES:

2 2-cup terrines or aluminum foil loaf pans

METHOD:

For this pâté you will need two bowls. Cut the pork and pork fat into large pieces and add them to the first bowl. Add the shallots and garlic and half the salt and pepper. Pour over half of the brandy and half the Madeira, mix thoroughly and set aside. Cut the ham and the veal into medium-size pieces and add to the second bowl. Pour over the remaining brandy, Madeira, salt, and pepper. Marinate the contents of these two bowls, covered, for three hours, stirring occasionally. At the end of the three hours, combine the two and put through the Cuisinart or food processor, medium grind. Then, add this mixture to one bowl. Add the eggs, one at a time and the parsley, and mix well. Get in there with your hands and really mix well! Line your terrines or aluminum foil pans with the strips of back fat. Add the pâté mixture, then cover with lids or aluminum foil. Place the terrines or loaf pans in hot water bath in a large rectangular pan and bake in a preheated 350° oven 1½ hours. When the pâtés are baked, remove from the oven and weigh down with a heavy plate and a can of tuna until set and cool enough to refrigrate. Refrigerate about 48 hours to allow the meats to "marry." Then serve or freeze.

PÂTÉ D'AMIENS
Wild Duck Pâté from the Somme

PREPARATION:

1 hour

COOKING TIME:

10 minutes at 400° and 1 hour and 50 minutes at 300°

INGREDIENTS:

Dough:
1 cup all-purpose flour
¼ pound unsalted butter
½ teaspoon salt
¼ cup cold water or more

1 wild duck,* with liver reserved
1 teaspoon butter
5 ounces bacon
¼ pound rabbit meat

* One pintail or mallard duck will supply a good-size breast; teal ducks are smaller and you will need two.

1 large egg, lightly beaten
¾ teaspoon salt
½ teaspoon freshly ground black pepper
½ 1-ounce can truffle peelings (optional)
2 tablespoons brandy
1 large egg yolk, lightly beaten with a little water

Duxelles Sauce:
4 medium mushroom caps
¼ medium yellow onion, finely chopped
½ tablespoon finely chopped shallots
¾ teaspoon salt
½ teaspoon freshly ground black pepper
¼ teaspoon nutmeg
1 tablespoon butter
1 tablespoon vegetable oil

MAKES:

1 5- to 7-inch round tart, approximately 6 slices

METHOD:

Dough:
Mix flour, salt and butter together in a bowl until crumbly (we use our fingers).
Add nearly all the water and mix. Add more water if needed. Do not overwork

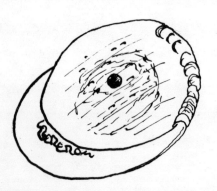

the dough. As soon as it forms a ball, even if it is not a smooth ball, stop and let it rest 30 minutes on a lightly floured breadboard. Then roll it out to make a 12-inch square. Fold the square in thirds, sides toward the center overlapping each other. Let the dough rest 10 minutes more under a well floured dish towel. Roll it again to a 12-inch square, fold it in thirds again then cover with floured towel until ready to use.

Remove the breast and any other nice pieces of meat from the duck and cut into finger-length pieces. Reserve for later use. Sauté the duck liver in one teaspoon sweet butter to harden it slightly, then set aside.

Duxelles Sauce:

Make the Duxelles Sauce by sauteéeing the mushrooms, onion, shallots, salt, pepper, and nutmeg in the butter and oil. Sauté this mixture until no juice is left. Set aside.

Finely grind the bacon, rabbit and cooked liver together in a Cuisinart or other processor. Add this mixture to a bowl to marinate for 30 minutes with the egg, salt, pepper, truffle peelings (if you wish) and brandy.

Roll out the dough you've made in advance into two circles, one circle 7 inches in diameter and the other 6 inches in diameter. Roll out the 7-inch circle to the thickness of a pie shell, a little more than ⅛ inch thick. Roll out the 6-inch circle a little thinner as it will be on the top. Put a layer of half the base (bacon, rabbit, liver) in the center of the larger circle. Then, add duxelles mixture in one layer. Next, add the layer of finger-length pieces of duck and cover with the other half of the base.

Sprinkle a little salt and pepper over the pâté mixture and place the 6-inch circle on top. There should be about one inch of the edge of the bottom circle showing. Brush this edge with water and turn it up all around to meet the top circle, rolling it up slightly. Press together to form a secure package. Make a hole about the size of a quarter in the center of the top. Brush the top with egg yolk and water mixed, and place on a cookie sheet covered with lightly buttered foil. Bake in a preheated 400° oven 10 minutes to brown, then reduce the heat to 300° and continue baking one hour and 50 minutes more. Serve hot as a first course or luncheon.

Paris and Pâtés

Henry IV lived in the Louvre in kingly opulence. Nevertheless, he had his maître d'hôtel go out to buy his favorite heron pâté from a pâté purveyor who lived on the left bank across from Notre Dame, where the Tour d'Argent restaurant stands today.

Parisians still follow the kingly tradition and buy their favorite regional pâtés from Brittany, the Loire valley, Auvergne, etc. at their neighborhood charcuterie. In spite of this convenience, many Parisian housewives insist upon making their own pâtés during the hunting season. If they prefer, however, they can take their wild game to the charcutier and he will transform their duck, pheasant, or even wild boar into pâté, paying himself *en nature* with a portion of the game meat for his own table. It is reassuring to find that someone's palate can still come before his pocketbook.

113

PÂTÉ MOUSSE AU BEURRE

PREPARATION:

30 minutes

COOKING TIME:

12 to 15 minutes

INGREDIENTS:

½ pound butter, softened
1 pound chicken livers
½ cup chopped yellow onions
2 tablespoons chopped shallots
¼ cup pared and chopped tart apple
¼ cup brandy
3 tablespoons heavy cream
1 teaspoon lemon juice
1 teaspoon salt
¼ teaspoon freshly ground black pepper
½ pound butter, clarified *

* Clarified butter: Melt 1 cup butter. Remove the pan from the heat and allow to sit for several minutes. Milky white particles will rise to the top and a clear yellow oil will settle to the bottom. Spoon off the milky residue. The clear yellow oil that remains is clarified butter.

MAKES:

1 2-cup terrine or 2 1-cup containers

METHOD:

Cut the butter into 16 equal size pieces (one tablespoon each). Wash and dry the chicken livers and cut in half. Chop the onion, shallots and apple by hand or place individually in a Cuisinart or other processor (using the S-shaped blade) and quickly chop. Melt 3 tablespoons of the butter in a skillet and sauté the onions 5 minutes. Add the apple and shallots and cook 2 minutes more. Place in a Cuisinart or other processor and blend thoroughly. Melt 3 more tablespoons of the butter in the same skillet and brown the chicken livers 3 to 4 minutes at a high heat. Add brandy and cook 2 minutes longer. Add the livers and juice to the other ingredients in the blender or Cuisinart and blend. Add the heavy cream and blend rapidly until very smooth. Place in a bowl and let cool to room temperature. You can set the bowl in a pan of cold water to hasten cooling. When cool, add the remaining 10 tablespoons softened butter to the mixture, along with the lemon juice, salt, and pepper. Mix thoroughly with a spoon and ladle into proper containers. Pour clarified butter over the top of each container, covering the top completely to form a good seal about ⅛ inch thick. Chill 2 hours or longer. Allow the pâté to nearly reach room temperature before serving, or cover with aluminum foil and freeze for later use. This is a very smooth, spreadable, delicate pâté. The butter topping should be eaten right long with the liver. Serve on saltine crackers as canapés and accompany with a dry red wine such as burgundy, zinfandel, or pinot noir.

CHICKEN LIVER PÂTÉ PARISIAN

PREPARATION:

1 hour

COOKING TIME:

2 hours at 350°

INGREDIENTS:

1½ pounds chicken livers
10 ounces pork or beef liver
12 ounces pork fat
 2 shallots, finely chopped
¼ cup finely chopped parsley
 1 large egg
¼ cup port
½ teaspoon allspice (scant)
¼ pound pistachios, shelled
 2 teaspoons salt
 2 teaspoons freshly ground black pepper
 1 teaspoon thyme
 1 thin (⅛″) piece of back fat, large enough to line your terrine and loaf pans
½ teaspoon tarragon
½ cup all-purpose flour, combined with 5 tablespoons water in a paste

MAKES:

1 3-cup terrine, 1 tiny aluminum foil loaf pan and 1 regular aluminum foil loaf pan
(8½ x 4½ x 2½)

METHOD:

Clean the chicken livers thoroughly, removing any dark spots and veins. Do the same with the pork or beef liver. Finely grind the chicken livers, pork or beef liver, and pork fat in your meat processor machine. Finely chop the shallots and parsley and place them together with the meats in a large mixing bowl. Add the egg, port, and allspice. Blanch the shelled pistachios in boiling salted water so they will retain their green color. Remove the skins. Add the blanched pistachios to the meat mixture along with the salt, pepper, and thyme. This terrine should be some-what spicy. Line your terrines or pans with the back fat, draping it over the sides both the width and length of the terrines. It should form a cross (see illustration). Fill with the meat base. This mixture will be rather thin but it firms up as it bakes Fold the back fat over the top, covering it completely. Sprinkle with the tarragon. Make a paste of flour and water and seal the lid of the terrine where it meets the bottom, all the way around, or cover your pans with aluminum foil. Put the terrine and loaf pans in a hot water bath in a large rectangular pan. Bake in a 350° preheated oven 1½ hours. Test for doneness by sticking a skewer or long needle into one of the pâtés covered with foil. If the tester comes out hot and the fat surrounding the pâtés is clear, they are baked. Leave the pans in their hot water bath to cool in the oven. Take them out when they are cool. Break the paste seal and remove the lids or foil. Weigh down with a heavy plate and can of tuna until the pâtés are completely cool. You can spread Aspic Jelly (pages 32–34) on top if you wish, then

117

refrigerate. This pâté is very spreadable and should keep two weeks in your refrigerator.

GÂTEAU DE CERVELLE

PREPARATION:

1 hour

COOKING TIME:

10 minutes to sauté
30 minutes to bake at 350°

INGREDIENTS:

  2 small calves' brains (frozen ones are fine)
  1 teaspoon wine vinegar
  1 medium yellow onion, finely chopped
  3 tablespoons vegetable oil
  3 tablespoons finely chopped parsley
  1½ tablespoons finely chopped chives
  ¼ cup dry vermouth or water
    Pinch of chervil
  1 teaspoon salt

¼ teaspoon freshly ground white pepper
6 large eggs
2 ounces pistachio nuts, blanched

MAKES:

1 medium soufflé dish (1½ quarts)

METHOD:

Soak the calves' brains in cold water to which you have added the vinegar. After they have soaked, remove the little red veins. Finely chop the parsley and chives. Pour the oil into a frying pan along with the chives, parsley, and onion and sauté about 5 minutes. Blanch the brains in boiling water 5 minutes, then remove, dry and put in the frying pan with the herbs. Pour the vermouth or water into the pan and simmer gently until all the liquid has evaporated. Cut the brains into large pieces. Beat 6 eggs as if you were making an omelette. Add the brains, the herb mixture from the frying pan, the chervil, salt, pepper, and pistachio nuts to the eggs. Pour this mixture into a well-buttered soufflé dish and bake in a hot water bath in a preheated 350° oven 30 minutes. Turn out on a platter a few minutes after removing from oven. Chill in the refrigerator and serve cold. This cakelike pâté is marvelous for luncheon or as a first course before dinner. Slice into wedges.

VEAU MARBRÉ

PREPARATION:

½ hour

COOKING TIME:

1½ hours at 350°

INGREDIENTS:

¼ cup dry white wine
 1 teaspoon unflavored gelatin
12 ounces leg of veal
12 ounces fatty shoulder of pork
 4 ounces pork fat
 2 large eggs
 1 tablespoon chopped chives or scallions
 1 teaspoon minced lemon peel
 2 teaspoons salt
 1 teaspoon freshly ground black pepper
 4 ounces tongue
 2 boneless chicken breasts
 1 thin (⅛″) piece back fat, large enough to line your terrine or loaf pans

MAKES:

1 medium terrine (1½ quarts) or loaf pan (8½ x 4½ x 2½)

METHOD:

Dissolve gelatin in two tablespoons of the wine and stir until dissolved. Bring the remaining 2 tablespoons of wine to a boil. Add the gelatin mixture and stir well, until the gelatin is completely dissolved. Put veal, pork, and pork fat in the Cuisinart or other processor and grind until fine. Place this ground meat into a bowl and add the eggs, chives, salt, lemon peel, and pepper and beat in the gelatin-wine mixture thoroughly. Cut the tongue and chicken breasts in finger-length strips and mix into the meat mixture well. Line a terrine or aluminum pan with back fat and pour in the pâté mixture. Cover with its lid or aluminum foil. Make one small slit with a knife on top of foil to allow steam to escape. Place terrine or loaf pans in a hot water bath in a large rectangular pan and bake in a preheated 350° oven 1½ hours or until the juices inside are clear when you remove the top. Let cool in the oven 20 minutes. Remove from the oven and weigh down with a heavy plate and can of tuna until it is completely cool, then refrigerate.

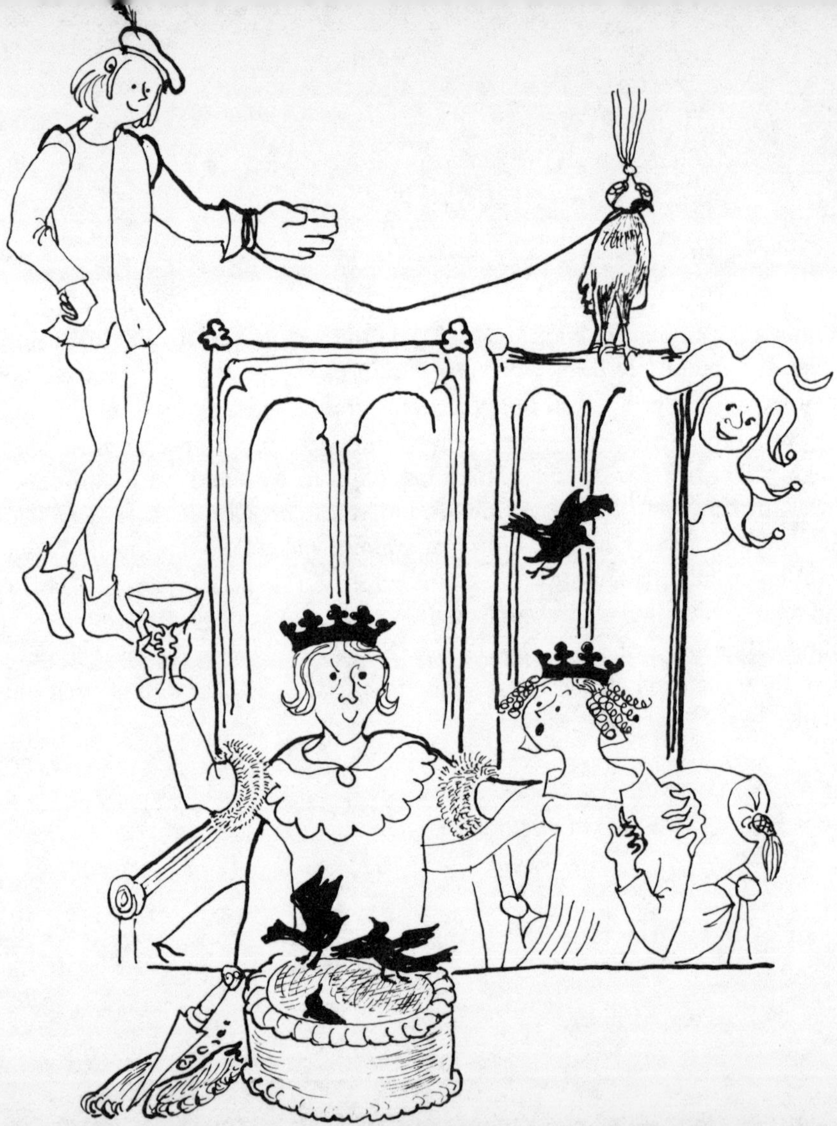

PASTIES

PASTIES, or meat pies, are the English cousins to pâté en croûte and the torte family. They probably were a fourteenth-century creation of the royal cooks of Richard II. A medieval reference, "pies were served that when open revealed little birds still hopping about inside," suggests that the old nursery rhyme, "Sing a Song of Sixpence," and its phrase "when the pie was opened, the birds began to sing" was a statement of fact. It was considered great sport to watch the king cut open his pasty releasing little birds as "fair" prey for the royal falcon. We shall leave the above recipe for the king, and for us commoners we include a classic Cornish pasty and one good English meat pie.

ENGLISH PASTY (Cornish)

PREPARATION:

30 minutes

COOKING TIME:

10 minutes at 400° and 50 minutes at 325°

INGREDIENTS:

Dough:
½ cup butter (soft, room temperature)
2 cups sifted all-purpose flour
½ teaspoon salt
½ to ¾ cup water

1 pound round steak, chopped or ground
1¼ cups chopped yellow onions
1 cup finely chopped raw potatoes
½ teaspoon salt
⅛ teaspoon freshly ground black pepper
1 tablespoon minced fresh parsley
2 tablespoons sweet butter
1 large egg yolk, combined with a little water
2 tablespoons heavy cream

MAKES:

8 first-course or 5 dinner-size pasties

METHOD:

Dough:

Use your fingers to work the butter, salt and flour together until crumbly. Make a hole in the center of the mixture and gradually pour in the water, mixing it together slowly. The dough should form a ball but not stick to the sides of the bowl or your fingers. Cover with plastic wrap and place in the refrigerator for at least 2 hours or overnight. Roll out the dough ⅛ inch thick and use a plain round cookie cutter to make 3-inch rounds (for hors d'oeuvres-size pasties) or 5-inch rounds (for luncheon- or dinner-size pasties).

Filling:

Combine the ground round, onion, potatoes, salt, and pepper. Then, place 2 to 3 tablespoons of the mixture in the center of each large round and 1 tablespoon in each small round. Sprinkle some minced parsley and a small bit of sweet butter on top. Moisten the entire edge of the dough and turn the dough over the filling to make a half-moon shape. Press the edges together firmly with a fork and prick the top several times. Brush the egg yolk-water mixture over the surface of the pasties. Place on a cookie sheet and bake in a preheated 400° oven 10 minutes. Reduce the heat to 325° and bake 50 minutes longer. About 15 minutes before the pasties should be done, remove them from the oven and cut a tiny slit in each top. Then, carefully pour a little heavy cream through a small funnel into each slit. (Kitchen parchment paper or heavy duty foil can be formed into a funnel.) Return the pasties to the oven and finish baking the last 15 minutes. Serve immediately.

PORK PIE FROM WARWICKSHIRE

PREPARATION:

15 minutes

COOKING TIME:

40 minutes at 425° and 1 to 1¼ hours at 350°

INGREDIENTS:

Dough:
- 2 cups all-purpose flour
- ½ pound unsalted butter
- 1 teaspoon salt
- ½ cup cold water or more

- 3 pounds fresh pork shoulder, boned and finely diced
- 2 tablespoons finely chopped yellow onion
- 2 teaspoons salt
- 1½ teaspoons freshly ground black pepper
- 1 tablespoon chopped fresh sage leaves or 1 teaspoon dried sage
- 2 cups chicken broth
- 1 large egg, lightly beaten
- 1 envelope unflavored gelatin

MAKES:

1 9- to 10-inch pie or 1 8 x 8 square Pyrex baking dish

METHOD:

Dough:

Mix flour, salt and butter together in a bowl until crumbly (we use our fingers)
Add nearly all the water and mix. Add more water if needed. Do not overwork th
dough. As soon as it forms a ball, even if it is not a smooth ball, stop and let it res
30 minutes on a lightly floured breadboard. Then roll it out to make a 12-inch square
Fold the square in thirds, sides toward the center overlapping each other. Let th
dough rest 10 minutes more under a well floured dish towel. Roll it again to a 12-inc
square, fold it in thirds again, then cover with floured towel until ready to use.

Filling:

Combine in a bowl the pork, onion, salt, pepper, sage, ¼ cup of the chicken brotl
and the egg. Roll out the dough and line the pan or dish with half the pastr
Pack with the meat mixture and cover with the remaining pastry. Cut a stear
hole in the center about the size of a quarter and bake in a 425° oven for 4
minutes with a cookie sheet on the shelf below the pie to catch any drips. Reduc
the oven temperature to 350° and continue cooking until the pie is quite browr
about 1 to 1¼ hours. Cover the pie with a piece of foil if you see that it is becomin;
too brown. Remove from the oven and allow to cool slightly. Soak the gelatin ii
¼ cup of the chicken broth. Heat to dissolve and add to the remaining 1½ cup.
broth. Spoon this gelatin mixture through a funnel (you can make a funnel out o

parchment paper or heavy-duty foil) into the steam hole on top of the pie. Remove pie from the pie plate, if possible, when it is cool. If this is too difficult, serve from the dish. This pie, which serves 8, should be offered at room temperature. It is delicious when served with a tart applesauce.

AMERICA'S MEAT LOAF

WHAT is American cuisine? To us, America is a dash of German, a teaspoon of Slavic, a sprinkle of Spanish, Oriental and middle Eastern, a pint of English, a soup-spoon of Russian, a cup of Irish and Scots, a pound of French and pinches of all the other countries that reflect our cultural blending. Mix well and you have America's standby—the meat loaf.

In its purest form the meat loaf closely resembles French pâté in its shape and use of ground meats and spices. It can also be served hot or cold like pâté, and can be stored for a period of time.

Every American cook has at least one good recipe for meat loaf in her repertoire, but we are including two variations on the theme just to show you that pâté has come full circle around the world.

CALIFORNIA MEAT LOAF

PREPARATION:

20 minutes

COOKING TIME:

50 minutes at 350° and 30 minutes at 250°

INGREDIENTS:

Sauce:
  1 cup olive oil
  1 cup finely chopped yellow onions
  ½ cup finely chopped parsley
  ½ cup chopped celery leaves
  4 cloves garlic, finely chopped

1 or 2 small hot chili(s), finely chopped
½ teaspoon marjoram
½ teaspoon oregano
  Salt to taste
2 cans (1 24-ounce and 1 9-ounce) peeled whole tomatoes
1 6-ounce can tomato paste

Meat Loaf:
  3 large eggs
2½ teaspoons salt
¼ teaspoon freshly ground black pepper
½ cup milk
  1 cup fresh bread crumbs
  2 pounds of ground veal, ground pork, and ground sirloin, in equal parts
¾ cup minced yellow onion
1½ cups finely chopped celery leaves
½ cup finely chopped parsley

MAKES:

1 large loaf, about 3 pounds

METHOD:

Sauce:
Pour the olive oil into a large pan. Sauté the onions lightly, about 20 minutes,

stirring constantly with a wooden spoon. Add the parsley, celery leaves, garlic, and chili(s). When lightly browned, add the marjoram, oregano, and salt. Simmer for one minute. Add the whole tomatoes and the tomato paste. Bring slowly to a boil and simmer for about ¾ of an hour. Stir often. If it gets too thick, add a little boiling water. It should have a nice consistancy so that when you pour it over the meat loaf it clings. This sauce freezes well and can be used for any number of other dishes.

Meat Loaf:
Beat eggs lightly and add the salt, pepper, milk, and bread crumbs. Combine with the ground meats, onion, celery leaves, and parsley, mix well, then form a loaf. Place in a well-greased (use bacon fat, if you have it) pan (12½ x 9 x 2). Bake in a pre-heated 350° oven 50 minutes. Then, pour a generous topping of the sauce over the meat loaf and bake 30 minutes more at 250°.

LAMB MEAT LOAF À L'INDIENNE

PREPARATION:

20 minutes

COOKING TIME:

1¼ hours at 350°

INGREDIENTS:

- 1 medium yellow onion, chopped fine
- 3 cloves garlic, pressed
- ½ cup chopped seedless raisins
- 3 pounds ground lamb ~~OR TURKEY~~ *LEAN BEEF*
- 1 large egg, lightly beaten
- ¼ cup pine nuts
- 1½ cups applesauce
- ¾ cup bread crumbs
- ½ cup dry red wine
- 1 tablespoon curry powder
- 1 teaspoon salt
- ¼ teaspoon freshly ground black pepper
- Chutney

IF MAKING HALF, USE 2 TSP CURRY, MORE PINE NUTS THAN ⅛ C, NOT TURKEY

MAKES:

1 large loaf, about 4 pounds

METHOD:

Chop the onion, garlic, and raisins by hand or in a Cuisinart or other processor. Place this mixture in a large bowl and add the lamb, egg, pine nuts, applesauce, bread crumbs, wine, curry powder, salt, and pepper. Shape into a large loaf and place in a buttered baking pan (13 x 9 x 2½). Bake in a preheated 350° oven 1¼ hours, uncovered. After the loaf has baked 35 minutes, drain off the fat in the pan and baste with some of the juice from the chutney bottle, using a basting brush. This will give the meat loaf a nice glaze. When baked, remove the loaf from the oven and let rest for 10 to 15 minutes before slicing. Serve with a side dish of chutney.

CORNICHON

THIS tiny vinegar pickle (gherkin) is the ideal accompaniment for any pâté. Because of the richness and flavors of pâté, a touch of sour sets it off beautifully. The cornichon should be nibbled rather than eaten whole and it brings out the full flavor of a pâté.

Jars of cornichons can be purchased from food specialty stores, but they are rather expensive. Therefore, we are providing a method for growing them yourself as well as an old French recipe for pickling them.

Cornichons are very easy to grow, as are all cucumbers, if you have sufficient sunshine and well-drained soil. Plant your seeds when the soil has warmed up enough for regular cucumber seeds, or start your seeds indoors in little pots and transplant later.

The plants should be trained up fences or wooden trellises, because they will be much easier to harvest and tend. If you do not have a garden plot, this little plant also thrives in an earthen pot or wooden box as long as the soil is sufficiently rich and the pot has good drainage. Set them on your patio, deck, or veranda in plenty of sun and train the vines up a wooden stake at least 6 to 8 feet tall. The pot should be 12 inches in diameter or larger. Plant 3 to 6 plants in each pot and as the vines appear, carefully train them upward.

Follow the package directions for correct watering procedures. When the flowers begin to appear, keep careful watch over the growth of the little cucumbers. Two inches maximum is the length of an authentic cornichon. Actually, slightly smaller is more desirable. As soon as your cucumbers reach this length, pick them and keep them in a storage bag in the refrigerator. When you have collected 35 pickles you are now ready to begin pickling.

Any small variety of cucumber can be used, but if you wish to use the real French seeds you can write to:

> J. A. Demonchaux Company
> 225 Jackson
> Topeka, Kansas 66603

Ask for the Fine Meaux or the Small Paris variety.
Or you may write to:

> W. Atlee Burpee Company
> 6350 Rutland Avenue
> Riverside, California 92502

Ask for West India Gherkin.

Recipe for Cornichon Pickles

Brush the cornichons with a good stiff brush to remove any spines or warts. Place a layer of cornichons in a large bowl. Add a layer of salt, then a layer of cornichons, and repeat until all pickles are used (35). Marinate them 24 hours and then drain well, wash and dry. Combine 1⅓ cups distilled white vinegar with ⅔ cup water, and bring to a boil. Cover the pickles with this liquid. Cover bowl and marinate another 24 hours. They should now be a yellow color. Pour off the liquid and bring it to a boil in a large pan. Add the cornichons and boil until they turn green again. When they are green, take them out, let them cool, then pack in hot sterilized half-pint or pint jars. Add some fresh tarragon if you have it, tiny white onions, green and red peppers sliced fine, garlic, and thyme. Pour the boiling vinegar mixture over the cornichons and seal with canning lids, which have also been scalded and are hot. Screw the rings down tightly and wipe off the jars. Set them out of a draft and allow them to cool. For a proper seal, the lids should make a "pop" sound and feel slightly indented. This recipe makes approximately 2 pints.

Pâté Picnic

GET away from it all in nature's dining room. The local park will do, or spread out a cloth on your rooftop, even on the living room floor. A picnic essentially should be a time of complete ease, and this is where pâté fits in so beautifully. Of course, it's made beforehand and waiting for you in the refrigerator. You can count on its being the stellar attraction of your picnic, as it is picnic fare par excellence. Before leaving, cut and butter long baguettes of French bread on which to serve thick slices of homemade pâté. Bring along one of your jars of cornichons and nicely chilled white or rosé wines—for kings, champagne. Include some little cherry tomatoes to dip in salt and pepper, hard-boiled eggs, and also plenty of *crudités*—carrots, celery, radishes, etc. For the next course, cheese (perhaps a Camembert or a large piece of dried Monterey Jack). For a finale, lots of fresh fruit. Try to keep your food light so you will be able to participate in post-picnic exercises.

A Ladies' Luncheon Pâté

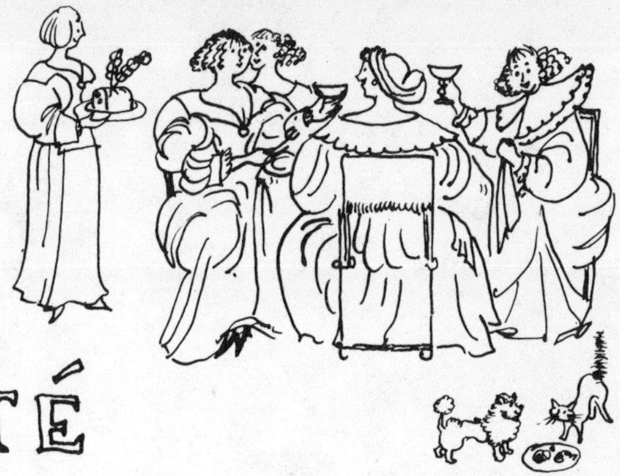

PÂTÉ in any form makes such an impressive luncheon dish. It pleases the eye, the palate and the waistline, and it eases your mind because it is not "last minute." Being intriguing fare, it shows your imaginaton as a hostess. Luncheon with the ladies, special friends, clients, or even the boss's wife becomes a special affair if you use pâté as the main course. Your guests will be impressed with a golden brown salmon koulebiaka accompanied by fresh broccoli or asparagus hollandaise or our Rabbit and Green Olive Pâté served with a leafy green salad, and fresh fruit for dessert. The Chicken Liver Cake from Normandy served in individual ramkins is particularly delicious with artichokes vinaigrette. And, for the "want-to-stay-slim" set, our Celery Root Pâté using the easy-to-make, fresh tomato sauce, is perfection.

Pâté Cocktail

THE typical American cocktail party is an all-encompassing affair. It can begin in the late afternoon and last an entire evening or merely serve as a prelude to an evening at the theater or dinner with friends. Whatever the reason for a cocktail *chez soi,* you might want several different and interesting hors d'oeuvres to accompany liquor and wine. If the traditional "chips and dips" have worn out their welcome, we would like to suggest pâté as a real solution to cocktail-party doldrums. It can be prepared days in advance, saving you last minute rush, and if you are planning a lengthy party, several variations can be served. For the short, intimate get-together, Pâté Mousse au Beurre with saltine crackers is ideal. For longer affairs, trays of pâtés, such as Pâté Parisian with Pistachios, Pâté Mousse with Bacon, Pâté Breton, or Pâté de Campagne G. Dumont, all served with plenty of French bread, sweet butter, and Cornichon pickles, make delicious offerings. Not only will your guests be delighted, but the heartier fare will prevent sleepiness, slurred speech, and boredom! Kirs (2 teaspoons of black currant liqueur in a wine glass, fill with chilled, dry white wine) and Bourguignons, (2 teaspoons of black currant liqueur in a wine glass, fill with room-temperature red burgundy) go well with these pâtés.

DINNER PÂTÉS

LET us imagine a dinner scene. You are the sun king, Louis XIV, and are very tired of dining in public with vast retinues of servants and staring courtiers who are not permitted to sit down. Instead, you have ordered a *trés petit couvert* to be sent to your private apartments in Versailles, enabling you to spend an *intime* evening. Your dining companion is just arriving at the bidden hour. The lovely young thing probably is one of many awaiting your royal command. The preset table with its fine linen, sparkling candelabra, and shimmering silver and crystal arrives, borne by liveried footmen and is presented before you. One of the many pâtés catches your blasé eye to the great relief of the lovely young thing who had assumed she was the entrée. We would like to think that either the Chicken Liver Cake with only blonde livers or the Cervelle Pâté could create this interlude. Cold Veal Pâté Maybelle, Veau Marbré, or Pâté du Canard à l'Orange will also create a touch of Versailles at your dinner table.

WINES

ANY memorable experiences await king and commoner alike when a fine pâté is complemented with an equally fine wine. The better gastronomic marriages can yield results on your palate ranging from pleasurable to exquisite. The ultimate decision as to which wine to select must be a matter of personal taste, yet the following guidelines should be of assistance. Keep in mind where the pâté will fit into your menu and what other wines and foods, if any, are being served. But above all, try to match the richness and sweetness of the pâté with the wine. Our pâtés can be generally categorized as follows:

CUSTARDLIKE PÂTÉS: With an egg binder; seasoned with chives, parsley, and chervil; these tend toward being very sweet, offering a light-bodied, yet very delicate taste that should be accentuated with an equally sweet and delicate white table wine. *France:* Select a sweet Vouvray, a Côte de Lyon, or from Alsace, a Riesling with a sweeter (*spätlese*) edge. *California:* a sweet Chenin Blanc, such as Mirassou, or a semisweet Chenin Blanc, such as Christian Brothers, Charles Krug, Inglenook, and Monterey Vineyards. Also attractive are the lighter-bodied sweet (late-harvest) white (Johannisberg) Rieslings, such as those produced by Chateau Montelena, Llords and Elwood, and Traubengold (Beringer). *Germany:* A 1971 or 1975 Spätlese from the Mosel-Saar-Ruwer area.

FISH AND VEGETABLE PÂTÉS: Seasoned with dill, chives, and chervil; tend toward a somewhat delicate semisweet taste. These are usually best mated with a comparable semisweet, light-bodied white or rosé wine. *France:* Muscadet, Pouilly-Fumé and Vouvray. *Germany:* A Qualitätswein, Kabinett, or Spatlese from the Nahe district. *Italy:* A fresh young (less than three years old) Frascati. *California:* White (Johannisberg) Riesling from Almaden, Beaulieu, Charles Krug, Heitz, Joseph Phelps, Mirassou, Robert Mondavi, Simi or Stags Leap Wine Cellars, or from St. Michelle (Washington State). Emerald Dry Riesling (Paul Masson); varietal rosés, such as rosé of Cabernet from Simi or Llords and Elwood, that have a sweet edge.

VEAL-BASED PÂTÉS: As well as those with ham, domestic rabbit and chicken are usually seasoned with laurel leaf, parsley, and shallots. They tend toward a bland flavor and fuller-bodied texture and thus can take fuller-bodied dry whites as well as good varietal rosés. *France:* Anjou-Rosé, Mâcon, Pouilly-Fuissé and

143

St. Veran. A young Beaujolais Villages can also fill the bill. *California:* Chardonnays from Beaulieu, Beringer, Chateau St. Jean, Heitz, Llords and Elwood, Monterey Vineyards, Robert Mondavi, Spring Mountain, Sterling, Geyser Peak; Fumé Blanc from Beringer, Mirassou and Robert Mondavi; Aurora Blanc: Bully Hill (New York State). Varietal rosés with a drier finish include Rosé of Cabernet from Buena Vista, Firestone Vineyards and Sterling. Gamay Rosés: the best are made by Robert Mondavi and Sutter Home. Zinfandel rosés come from Concannon and Pedroncelli. Petite rosé from Mirassou. Rosé of Pinot Noir: Firestone.

PORK-BASED PÂTÉS: Including liver, heart, and melt; tend to be darker colored and are frequently seasoned with thyme, peppercorns, garlic, and onion. They offer up lusty, hearty, full-bodied tastes. Sometimes they are laced with brandy or fortified wines such as Madeira or port. Thus, light- to medium-bodied red wines are called for. *France:* From Bordeaux, seek out a Médoc, Graves, St. Emilion, or Pomerol. From Burgundy choose a lighter-bodied Volnay, Santenay or a Beaune. A medium-bodied wine, such as Chambertin, Nuits-St. Georges, Vosne-Romanée, or a Clôs Vougerot. *Italy:* Seek out D.O.C. wines, such as Gattinara or Ghemme. *Spain:* Red Rioja. *California:* Zinfandels from Buena Vista, Heitz, Charles Krug, Louis Martini, Robert Mondavi, Château Montelena, Sebastiani, and Sutter Home. Pinot Noir from Beaulieu, Hoffman Mountain Ranch, Llords and Elwood, Robert Mondavi, Sebastiani, and Stonegate. Merlot from Sterling. Pinot St. George (red Pinot) from Christian Brothers and Inglenook. Cabernet Sauvignons from Louis Martini or Charles Krug. *New York State:* Boordy Red and Bully Hill Red.

PÂTÉS FROM WILD GAME: Pheasant, duck, and hare are very robust and full bodied. *France:* Seek out a Châteauneuf-du-Pape, Côte Rôtie or Hermitage or a red Bordeaux. *Italy:* Barolo or Chianti. *California:* A full-bodied Cabernet Sauvignon, such as Beaulieu, Freemark Abbey, Robert Mondavi, Parducci, or Spring Mountain. Petite Sirahs from Concannon, David Bruce, Fortino, Mirassou, Parducci, Souverain of Rutherford, Inglenook or Cresta Blanca.

CHICKEN-LIVER-BASED PÂTÉS: These tend to fall into two groups. While smooth in texture and frequently flavored with shallots, onion, bacon, thyme, bay leaves, and brandy, the pronounced liver taste usually remains on the palate. Those with considerable additions of bacon fat, butter and truffles can approach the richness of foie gras, and thus require the richer, full-bodied wines recommended for foie gras. Use of light to moderate amounts of bacon and butter will yield a considerably less rich pâté. These are more on the style and richness level of pork-based pâtés, and call for the light- to medium-bodied red wines suggested above for pork pâtés.

FOIE GRAS: This quintessence of buttery richness (with or without French black truffles) is in a class by itself and you usually need a rich, very sweet white wine. *France:* Select the best and richest Sauterne, Barsac, or Monbazillac. *Germany:* Consider a fine Rhinegau or Rhinehessen Auslese (1969 or 1971). *California:* Select a very rich, full-bodied, late harvest white wine such as White (Johannisberg) Riesling from Château St. Jean (select late harvest), Beringer (Knights Valley Auslese), Wente (Spätlese or Auslese), or a late harvest Riesling from Joseph Phelps or Freemark Abbey.

Index

147

148